LEADING FROM THE EAST

Innovative Strategies for Masonic Lodges

CHRISTOPHOR J. GALLOWAY
PAST MASTER OF VALLEY-HI LODGE 1407

Copyright © 2024
CHRISTOPHOR J. GALLOWAY
PAST MASTER OF VALLEY-HI LODGE 1407
LEADING FROM THE EAST
Innovative Strategies for Masonic Lodges
All rights reserved.

No part of this publication may be reproduced, distributed, or transmitted in any form or by any means, including photocopying, recording, or other electronic or mechanical methods, without the prior written permission of the author, except in the case of brief quotations embodied in critical reviews and certain other non-commercial uses permitted by copyright law.

CHRISTOPHOR J. GALLOWAY
PAST MASTER OF VALLEY-HI LODGE 1407
Perfect Ashlar Publishing.
Universal City, TX

Printed Worldwide
First Printing 2024
First Edition 2024

ISBN: 978-1-7362557-0-4 (Print)
ISBN: 978-1-7362557-1-1 (eBook)

10 9 8 7 6 5 4 3 2 1

For permission requests, email to the publisher, addressed "Attention: Permissions Coordinator," at the email address below.

For ordering information please visit Perfect Ashlar Publishing's website at: www.PerfectAshlarPublishing.com

All Scripture quotations marked NIV are taken from the Holy Bible, New International Version NIV Copyright 1973, 1978,1984,2011 by Biblica, Inc. Used by permission of Zondervan. All rights reserved worldwide. www.zondervan.com. The NIV and New International Version are trademarks registered in the United States Patent and Trademark Office by Biblica.

Scriptures Marked KJV are taken from the King James Version (KJV) King James Version public domain.

DEDICATION

This book is dedicated to my family. They have been my support from the time of my Masonic journey to the East and beyond. Especially my wife, Kimberly, who has always been a pillar for me to lean on.

To the Brothers of Valley-Hi Lodge for believing in me and trusting me with the gavel to guide our Blue Lodge. Thank you to all the Past Masters who whispered good counsel into my ear.

Finally, this book is dedicated to Freemasonry. Without our fraternity, having the experiences and meeting the Brothers that have changed my life would not have been possible.

JUST ONE EXAMPLE

Within this book, I share my perspectives and experiences of leading one Blue Lodge. The contents of this book do not represent any Grand Lodge positions or recommendations. The reader should keep in mind that the Blue Lodge discussed in this book is located in Texas, and therefore, all the rules and regulations that this Blue Lodge follows are under the Grand Lodge of Texas' jurisdiction.

Therefore, before attempting to implement any of the recommendations presented in this book, Blue Lodge leaders should review their Grand Lodge laws and Blue Lodge's bylaws, rules, and regulations. Some suggestions in this book may be controversial, and some readers may feel uncomfortable with the advice and experiences within the pages of this book. Each reader must carefully consider their members' needs and the Blue Lodge before making any changes or implementing new ideas.

TABLE OF CONTENTS

Foreword 1
Introduction 3
   Journey to the East 3
Chapter 1 7
   Freemasonry's Quiet Revolution
      Push and Pull Factors 8
      Engaging New Generations 8
      How to Use This Book 11
Chapter 2 13
   The 21st Century Worshipful Master
      Volunteer Leadership 14
      Transformational Leadership 16
      Are Masonic Lodges a Business? 19
Chapter 3 21
   Establish a Why
      The Golden Circle 21
      Possible Grand Lodge Golden Circle 24
      Possible Blue Lodge Golden Circle 24
      Always Start With Why 25
Chapter 4 26
   Organization Goals
      Valley-Hi Lodge #1407 Goals 26
      Valley-Hi Lodge #1407 Officers-Elect Meeting 27
Chapter 4 29
   Goal #1, Lodge Sustainability
      Dues and Degree Fees 29
      Endowments to Sustain a Lodge 40
      Organization Procedures and Rules 43
      Membership Recruiting 44
      Lodge History 54

Chapter 5 59
   Goal #2, Lodge Facilities
      First Impressions 60
      Analysis Paralysis 61
      A New Approach 67
      Pitching In 73
Chapter 7 77
   Goal #3, Education
      Philanthropy 77
      Local Elementary & Orphanage 80
      Scholarships 80
      Masonic Education 81
      Brother-Compiled List of Masonic Podcasts 84
Chapter 8 94
   Heavy is the Crown
      Lodge Officers 94
      Past Masters 99
      Full Responsibility 100
      Modeling Leadership 103
A Call to Action 106
Leading From the East 107
Recommended Reading List 108
About the Author 111
A Note To The Reader 113
Notes 130

Foreword

In my nine-plus years on the Texas Committee for Masonic Education and Service and teaching the Officer Leadership Training program, any time I visited a Lodge, it was always evident to me whether the Worshipful Master had attended the OLT program or not. All the knowledge and instruction presented in the OLT programs are designed to give Lodge officers the ability and confidence to make a difference, not only in their Lodges but also in themselves and Freemasonry.

In this book, Brother Galloway has expertly woven the OLT lessons into the story of his year as Worshipful Master of his Lodge. That is not to say everything he learned was from the Officer Leadership Training classes, as his background and experience show his previous aptitude in leadership, planning, and management. Much of the OLT was, in many ways, a reinforcement of those strengths. Brother Galloway took this knowledge and added the last and maybe the most critical piece of the puzzle, which is desire and energy, and transformed a regular Masonic Lodge into a vibrant, energetic, focused team of Brothers, each doing his part for the betterment of the Lodge.

This book incorporates all the elements of a profitable business, or in this case, a good Lodge, and lays out a step-by-step blueprint for success. Yes, this book's beauty is that he doesn't just tell the reader what to do; Brother Galloway explains precisely how to do it.

Readers will learn how to gain buy-in and consensus from the members, plan significant projects, analyze the Lodge's financial health and future, and successfully leverage community involvement. Additionally, this book offers the proper and efficient use of social media to attract new members to new ideas and Masonic Education sources. The reader can expect all this and much, much more.

I found the book both instructional and entertaining and a veritable textbook on Lodge transformation and success as a Worshipful Master. I am sure you will enjoy it.

James C. "Chris" Williams IV

PM Davy Crockett Lodge No. 1225

Brother Williams is Past Master of Davy Crockett Lodge No. 1225 in San Antonio, TX, and several other Lodges. He holds membership in the Scottish Rite Valley of San Antonio, the York Rite, and the Shrine.

As a member of the Grand Lodge of Texas Masonic Education and Service Committee, Brother Chris has, for the last nine years, assisted in the instruction of prospective officers in the revitalization, administration, and management of their Lodges. He has spoken at lodges and Masonic gatherings all over Texas on various topics, from History to Grand Lodge Law to our Degrees' philosophy and symbolism and much more. He has an enduring love of Masonic education and is committed to spreading Masonic light whenever and wherever possible.

Introduction

Journey to the East

"We can only know the fullest joys of Masonry when we truly walk the paths of service and of hard work in the quarries."

– George E. Burow 33°

It is difficult to recall when the Freemasons were first introduced to me. It may have been some blockbuster movie or a conspiracy TV show. Even though I did not know it at the time, my memory of when I met my first Freemason is clear.

When I was eleven years old, we moved to my step dad's hometown in Illinois. There, I met his father, Frank Galloway. Unfortunately, Frank had a stroke ten years before we met. He was paralyzed on the left side of his body and could not speak. There were two things that I noticed about him; he loved his St. Louis Cardinals, and he had a cool "Galloway" ring that he never took off. By now, you most likely have already realized that his ring was a Square and Compasses ring with the letter "G" in the center. In my young mind, the G stood for "Galloway."

Fast forward eight years, sitting at his funeral, I observed several men in attendance. Towards the end of the service, our neighbor, who spent countless hours with my grandfather, stood up and announced that Brother Frank Galloway was a Freemason. He asked us to step outside of the service briefly. When we returned, several of the men were wearing aprons. There was a brief presentation and a Masonic Burial Service for my grandfather. The respect that the Masons had for my grandfather had a profound impression on me.

As a twenty-year-old man, I was then living in Texas and definitely not mature enough to knock upon a lodge door. Life happened. I got married and had two beautiful children. A decade passed, and I separated from my first wife. One evening while I was in my one-bedroom apartment feeling like I had hit rock bottom, I began to think about my life and the connection that my grandfather had to those men, even in death. A simple Google search led me to the websites for two lodges that were close to my apartment. That night, I emailed both lodges the following email:

On Aug 29, 2013, at 12:00 am, Chris Galloway wrote:

Subject: Membership Information?

> Hello,
>
> My name is Chris Galloway. I would like some information about becoming a member of your lodge. My grandfather, Frank Galloway, was a Mason in Illinois.
>
> He has passed away, so I don't know of any Masons. I'm not sure what steps I need to take. I would strongly appreciate your guidance. I look forward to hearing back from you. Thank you for your time.
>
>
> Respectfully,
>
> Chris Galloway.

Two days later, the secretary from Valley-Hi Lodge #1407, where I eventually served as the Worshipful Master, responded to my email. The other lodge never responded. I am relatively confident that there would have been a good chance that I would have joined the other lodge because it was geographically closer to my apartment. Having a sound communication system and following up in a timely manner was the first lesson that I would carry with me on my way to the East.

In February of 2014, I was initiated into the fraternity, assigned a mentor, and began my work as an Entered Apprentice. After eleven months, I completed the requirements of the first two degrees and was raised to the sublime degree of a Master Mason in January of 2015. When lodge officer elections came up in June, as a very green Master Mason, I officially began my journey to the East by being elected to Junior Deacon.

Some readers may be entirely "shocked" that a newly raised Brother would be elected to an officer position, while the majority of you may have seen this time and time again in your lodge. Our lodge is no different from most. There are approximately 115 members on our books. Despite these numbers, at the time of my raising, there were less than 20 Master Masons that attend lodge regularly, and the Worshipful Master was serving his second consecutive year in the East. The members of our lodge worked hard to fill positions to ensure that I did not skip any chairs on my journey. To do this, the lodge members elected two members from one of our sister lodges to a plural membership and then to Senior Warden. Both also served our lodge as Worshipful Master. Additionally, our Worshipful Master, the year I was Junior Deacon, served a second year in the East when I was the lodge's Junior Warden. My year as the lodge's Senior Warden, the Worshipful Master was a Past Master from before my initiation into the lodge.

The purpose of sharing the preceding details is to give some insight into my journey and the difficulties that our lodge faced. After being raised to the sublime degree of a Master Mason, there is no honor more significant than being asked to serve as the Worshipful Master of a Blue Lodge. With great humility, the honor was bestowed to me in the summer of 2019. As the Senior Warden, my biggest fear was my inexperience as a Mason might lead to failure as the Worshipful Master, and the Brothers might be disappointed with their choice.

Quickly, it became evident that while experience as a Mason is essential, it was the professional experiences that were critical in my year. Time will be the judge of the legacy that was forged during my twelve months of service to the lodge. Chances are you have contemplated the legacy that you want to leave behind. Hopefully, this book will be a valuable resource on your journey of leading and improving your lodge. The contents of this book will hopefully provide current, future, and Past Masters with some sound advice, tools, and resources to help them on their Masonic journey while sitting in the East or inspire an idea to improve their lodge. If this book provides readers with at least one thing they can use, or dare I say one thing not to do, then it has served its purpose.

Chapter 1

Freemasonry's Quiet Revolution

"If Freemasonry is able successfully to conclude its 'quiet revolution,' while at the same time ensuring that its central features are retained to preserve the true 'spirit' of Freemasonry, then its future may well be assured – for the next century or two at least."

- SIRC, 2012

In 2012, the Grand Secretary of the United Grand Lodge of England (UGLE) enlisted the help of the Social Issues Research Centre (SIRC) to conduct a research study on Freemasonry. The study's purpose was to portray to the public that the UGLE is a transparent organization. The SIRC is an unaffiliated, unbiased, and reputable United Kingdom-based research organization that was tasked with determining if there is a need and future for Freemasonry.[1] During the research study, known Freemasons and unaffiliated men and women citizens of the UK were interviewed. The interview questions centered around three research topics; Bonding, Giving, and Ritual. During the interviews with members of the fraternity, the term "quiet revolution" was referenced.[2] Quiet revolution is used to describe the fraternity's internal struggle with the need to modernize to meet today's societal demands.

Push and Pull Factors

There is a push within Freemasonry to make progressive changes that will engage the next generation of Master Masons. A Google search of the keywords "Freemasonry in the 21st Century" will yield blog posts and articles on the need to modernize the fraternity and change the current practices. This push is mostly from younger Masons that feel their lodge is not meeting their needs. Likewise, the same Google search will result in articles advocating that Freemasonry should be left unchanged.

The pull factor is mostly the fraternity's older members who want to hold on tightly to the Craft and lodge traditions. While both sides of the debate can agree that the fraternity's rituals (e.g., esoteric work, the degrees) should remain in their original form, some innovative ideas and practices can overall improve the Blue Lodge. Current or future Worshipful Masters should be fully aware of the push and pull factors that may arise in their lodge. Worshipful Masters should also consider alternative approaches to lodge traditions or practices (e.g., leadership, operations, education, marketing) as a way to move the Blue Lodge into the 21st century.

Engaging New Generations

This book serves several different purposes:

1. To provide a model of how, as Worshipful Master, I improved my lodge and potentially solidified its future by applying innovative leadership strategies.

2. It encourages readers to seek more light in leadership practices and strengthen their lodge, and it aims to reengage readers into their Blue Lodge.

3. This book is also a call to action that a new approach must be taken to keep Freemasonry around for another 300 years.

For over 200 years, Masonic scholars have written about the need for innovation and Freemasonry to "save our fraternity." However, this message is different.

In the early 1900s, several technological advances benefited people. Transportation made great strides over the last hundred years, and now people can be around the world within a matter of a few hours. The telegraph and the telephone inventions made it easier for people to connect across the world and have in-depth conversations. The radio and television provided entertainment for people who could be entertained in their homes without traveling anywhere. Despite all these inventions, with each generation, there was still a need to belong to something better than themselves. There was a need to engage with human beings face-to-face to roll up their sleeves and help their neighbor and community. Freemasonry benefited by fulfilling the need to connect, self-improve, and be charitable for over 300 years. Throughout recent history, Freemasonry has continued to be a fraternity that is sought out and enjoyed by millions of men worldwide.

As our older members put down their working tools and join the Grand Architect of the Universe, our membership ranks continue to decline. Freemasonry's future depends on the Blue Lodge's ability to attract the new generations that need to fill our dwindling ranks.

However, the challenge is that these new generations (X generation, the millennial generation, and generation Z) have witnessed a different type of technological advances than our Brothers of the past. These new generations have seen the explosion of social media and smart technology. Today, younger generations can receive information instantaneously. There is no need to leave the house to pick up a newspaper, turn on the TV or radio. The X, millennial, and Z Generations have the same needs that our past Brothers had, but today they can satisfy those exact needs with a computer or iPhone in the palm of their hand.

Young adults today can sit in a recliner in the comfort of their home, open up a laptop, start a charity with a GoFundMe page, post a link on their social media account, and within a matter of hours, raise thousands of dollars and in some rare cases, millions of dollars for any charity or for any cause they see fit. They can communicate through texting, social media, Twitter post, blogs, or any number of outlets without leaving their home. Today's technology has filled their need to give back or connect with another human being.

Now more than ever, it is imperative that Masonic lodges take a serious look at how they want to attract and keep the future Brothers of tomorrow. Blue Lodge leaders need to consider what their lodge's brand is going to be. Will it be community support through philanthropy, will it be Masonic education meant to help men become better men, will it be Brotherly love and building connections, or any other noteworthy undertaking?

Within the pages of this book, there are resources and examples of strategies that can help the leadership of your Blue Lodge identify your vision, attract new members from several generations, and engage your lodge to keep the new members who join. Additionally, the very same strategies will help reengage Brothers who have disengaged from the Blue Lodge.

How to Use This Book

While this book has several examples of how, as Worshipful Master, I applied innovation to improve my Blue Lodge, this book is not a cookie-cutter blueprint of how a lodge should be operated. I hope that readers will visualize the overall thought process and strategies that our Blue Lodge leadership used to formulate a strategic plan for moving into the future. Several references to outside resources helped inform this book's content and are referred to throughout. Hopefully, this book will serve as an inspiration to future and current Worshipful Masters to seek additional light on how to be great leaders, which will allow them to apply innovative strategies to improve their Blue Lodge. For Past Masters, this book will also serve as inspiration for you to become more engaged in your lodge and provide guidance and mentorship to your lodge's Worshipful Masters and future leaders.

Keep an open mind about what you will find throughout this book. Reflect on what you read and consider how it could be applied to your lodge or what new innovative ideas and practices you or your leadership team can develop to make improvements. It is highly encouraged to share what is in this book with your Blue Lodge leadership team and other Masons you respect and trust. Reflection and collaboration are genuinely the only ways to internalize and best apply any new knowledge gained.

I wish you luck on your journey to better your lodge and in Freemasonry. Do not hesitate to share your successes and struggles on our website and blog at www.PerfectAshlarPublishing.com.

Chapter 2

The 21st Century Worshipful Master

"If you want to lead, you need to grow. Good Leaders are always good learners."

– John C. Maxwell.

In the early 2000s, there was a popular television show called The West Wing that each week took viewers into the White House. There is a powerful scene from an episode[3] where President Bartlett invited his boyhood priest, Father Cavanaugh, to the Oval Office to guide him through a difficult decision. Upon entering the Oval Office, Father Cavanaugh tells the President that he does not know how to address him.

Father Cavanaugh: "I don't know how to address you. Would you prefer Jed or Mr. President?"

President Bartlett: "To be honest, I prefer Mr. President."

Father Cavanaugh: "That's fine."

President Bartlett: "You understand why, right?"

Father Cavanaugh: "Do I need to know why?"

President Bartlett: "It's not ego."

Father Cavanaugh: "I didn't think it was."

President Bartlett: "There are certain decisions that I have to make while I'm in this room. Do I send troops into harm's way? Which federal agency gets the most research money? It's helpful in those situations to not think of yourself as the man, but as the Office."

Father Cavanaugh: "Then Mr. President it is."

The memory of this episode came flooding back a few days before my installation into the East. As the President of the United States, the office has great power, so does the Worshipful Master of a Blue Lodge. The Brother who accepts the honor to lead his Blue Lodge should not push his agenda but should rule from the perspective that he represents all the Brethren of the lodge. The Worshipful Master has the power to enact wonderful things for his lodge. Consequently, a Worshipful Master that does not understand his responsibilities to the lodge, or worse yet is power-hungry, can also destroy it.[4] Therefore, any Brother who is hoping to serve in the progressive line should take the time to research and understand the best practices to lead a 21st century Blue Lodge.

Volunteer Leadership

Freemasonry is unique in that it is built and led by volunteers. Volunteers can choose to engage, not engage, or walk away at any time. This poses a challenge for Worshipful Masters that need to meet the members' needs, follow Grand Lodge Law, and keep the doors open. Despite being the final authority on all things in the Blue Lodge, the Worshipful Master must be a collaborative leader to move the organization forward. Ruling with a heavy gavel will surely disengage the Master Masons and drive away Entered Apprentices who are quietly observing from the sidelines.

> Because of the Worshipful Master's sovereign authority and power within the lodge proceedings, a person with little or no leadership qualities or training will be very ineffective in conducting the lodge affairs and accomplishing the many objectives and tasks that must be done during the year. However, a Worshipful Master who can organize his plans for the year, can envision the obstacles of manpower, monetary needs, time restraints, etc., and can enlist the help of other lodge members to work in a unified force toward achieving the goals, will have a very successful and enjoyable year as Worshipful Master, and the lodge will benefit.5

In his article on Masonic Leadership, Brother Freeman identified three leadership styles as most effective in a volunteer organization or Blue Lodge. These three leadership styles are:

1. The **Sharing Leader**. This type of leader is a collaborator and effective delegator—an influencer who knows how to motivate the lodge leadership and members into action.

2. The **Reconciling Leader**. This Worshipful Master is a relator and is engaged in maintaining peace and harmony among the Brethren. He may not complete many projects in his year, but he will build a strong culture within the lodge that will be primed for the next Worshipful Master to call the Brothers to action.

3. The **Building Leader**. This leader is a manager—a Worshipful Master who will maintain the progress from the previous year. There is no burning need to implement

change. The Worshipful Master's focus is to pass on the gavel at the end of his year with the lodge in better shape than he received it, but as long as the lodge is not in worse condition, his mission was accomplished.[6]

According to Brother Freeman, the most effective of the three leadership styles identified above is the Sharing Leader.[7] However, the most influential leader in any organization is the executive, who can be the leader that the organization needs. Therefore, the Worshipful Master who can apply a combination of multiple leadership styles will be the most effective leader. Worshipful Masters must differentiate their leadership style and approach to the lodge's needs, individual members, and situation as it arises. A one-size-fits-all approach will not move a lodge forward in the 21st century. Freemasonry needs transformational leaders to keep the fraternity around for another 300 years. Every lodge is unique because each Brother, who is a member, is also unique.

Transformational Leadership

Transformational Leadership occurs when "leaders and followers" push each other and "advance to a higher level of morale and motivation."[8] Transformational Worshipful Masters effectively evaluate their lodge and can apply the appropriate leadership styles to any given situation. Additionally, other qualities make someone a successful transformational leader. According to Bernard M. Bass's Transformational Leadership Theory, four components make up transformational leadership.[9]

1. A transformational Worshipful Master, through **Intellectual Stimulation**, inspires his leadership team and the Brethren to think creatively about the Blue Lodge and how they can progressively improve their lodge.

2. Through **Individual Consideration**, a transformational Worshipful Master fosters a relationship with each individual. He creates an environment that is safe for Brothers to speak up and share ideas. Each person is viewed as a leader who has something they can offer to the Blue Lodge.

3. Transformational Worshipful Masters have a clear vision for the direction of their year in the East. He can communicate that vision to the Brethren, and using **Inspirational Motivation**; he guides the Brothers to embracing the same goals.

4. As a model leader, the Transformational Worshipful Master gains the Brethrens' trust and respect by leading from the front with compassion. His **Idealized Influence** results in the other Brothers emulating his passion and leadership in the Blue Lodge.

It can be overwhelming thinking about the many leadership styles and qualities that make up a highly effective Worshipful Master, but you already have the most critical piece. While the four characteristics above are qualities of a transformational leader, the most important one is not listed; **Heart**. A compassionate heart the foundation that will help you grow into a transformational leader. The second piece to that puzzle is a willingness to learn what it takes to become the best Worshipful Master that you can be. The mere fact that you are reading this book proves that you are willing to grow as a leader.

Whether your time in the East is in the past, present, or near future, or you lead your lodge in another way, it is never too late to begin refining your leadership style. Tap into Masonic and non-Masonic leadership books, podcasts, and articles about building your leadership toolbox. Practice the strategies learned at work and within your Blue Lodge. Do not be discouraged by the genre (e.g., business, education, or religion) of the leadership book or podcasts because there are golden nuggets in every book that can be applied to any environment, including Freemasonry. Here are a few quotes from leadership books that have shaped my leadership style over the years.

> "The true price of leadership is the willingness to place the needs of others above your own. Great leaders truly care about those they are privileged to lead and understand that the true cost of the leadership privilege comes at the expense of self-interest.
>
> And when a leader embraces their responsibility to care for people instead of caring for numbers, then people will follow, solve problems and see to it that that leader's vision comes to life the right way, a stable way, and not the expedient way."
>
> — **Simon Sinek,** *Leaders Eat Last: Why Some Teams Pull Together and Others Don't*

> "Decision making brings together many of the finest traits of contrarian leadership—thinking gray, thinking free, artful listening, delegating authority while retaining ultimate responsibility, artful procrastination, ignoring sunk costs, taking luck into account, and

listening to one's inner voice. Weaving these traits together is an art itself. When it is done well, the result is a thing of beauty and a powerful tool for effective leadership."

— **Steven B. Sample,** *The Contrarian's Guide to Leadership*

"When leaders teach, they invest in their people's ability to solve and avoid problems in the future."

— **Liz Wiseman,** *Multipliers, Revised and Updated: How the Best Leaders Make Everyone Smarter*

Despite being from books focused on business and educational leadership, the above quotes crossover and can be applied in any organization. There are Masonic books that have tackled the topic of adapting different genres of books to benefit Freemasonry. In 2018 Brothers Robert Johnson & Jon Ruark explained how a lodge could adapt well-known corporate leadership strategies and apply them to Blue Lodge operations.[10] Any Brother who is passionate about Blue Lodge leadership should explore a wide variety of leadership books that they can adapt to their Masonic leadership experience.

Are Masonic Lodges a Business?

After so many business leadership references, this may be a question that has crossed your mind. It is a valid question, so let's reflect on it. A business has a mission, a customer base, a product, generates revenue, and has expenses. A lodge has a mission (to make good men better men), a customer base (the members of the lodge), a product (Masonry, fellowship, education), and it generates revenue (dues, degree fees, raises money through fundraising). It has expenses (supplies, utilities, repairs, rent). It does appear that the Blue Lodge is a business, and like any business, it can fail without the proper leadership or intervention when necessary.

What would happen to a business if the CEO was replaced with a new person to lead the organization every year? How successful would that same business be if each year the priorities of the organization changed? Now, imagine if that new executive leadership team had no business experience. There would be a strong possibility that business would not survive for too much longer.

My Brother, this was not meant to trifle with your feelings. It was not meant to discredit any past, current, or future Worshipful Master who has never led a business. The point is that current or future Worshipful Masters can all benefit from the research of leadership books outside of Masonry to guide them while in the East. The next chapter focuses on the business approach we adapted to benefit Valley-Hi Lodge.

Chapter 3

Establish a Why

"All organizations start with WHY, but only the great ones keep their WHY clear year after year."

— Simon Sinek.

Every person and every organization must establish a Why. A Why is emblematical of purpose, or reason, for existence. Establishing a lodge's why guides the members to determine the organization's mission and vision. Goals that are created by the lodge should support the organization's mission, vision, and ultimately reflect the Why.

For Masonic lodges, establishing a viable Why is significant because each year, there are leadership changes that can derail the progress that is made if the new leadership fails to understand the lodge's purpose.

The Golden Circle

In his book, *Start With Why: How Great Leaders Inspire Everyone To Take Action*, motivational speaker Simon Sinek outlined the importance for organizations to establish and understand their purpose. He used his Golden Circle to reflect how leaders and organizations establish their Why, How, and What. The Golden Circle is an adaptation of the Golden Ratio, which is a mathematical based formula that can be traced back through history as a tool successfully used by practitioners within the seven liberal arts.

According to Sinek, human biology has an impact on what motivates someone to be loyal or draws people to an organization. Our fraternity depends on men to be drawn to our organization and to be loyal Brothers. Without those two things, our fraternity will eventually cease to exist. A detailed explanation can be found in Sinek's article Concepts of Golden Circle, and on YouTube, there is a great video of Sinek's presentation on the Golden Circle. Masonic Grand Lodges and individual blue lodges can benefit from Sinek's work.[11] Figure 1 below is a graphic of Sinek's Golden Circle with his example for Apple.

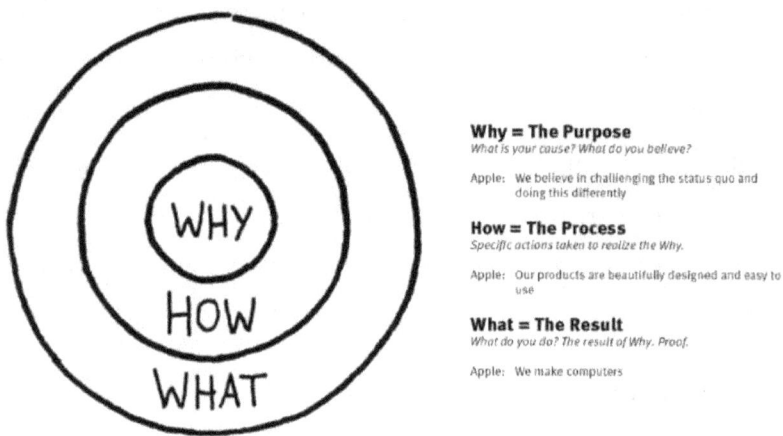

Figure 1: Reprinted from Concepts of the Golden Circle, Simon Sinek (2016)

When an organization develops the Why, How, What, Vision, Mission, or Goals, it should be in collaboration with the stakeholders. The stakeholder representation of a Masonic lodge would be the officers, members, and possibly a community member or organization that the lodge frequently has an impact on. It is critical that, at the very least, the Worshipful Master, Senior Warden, and Junior Warden are the officers represented on the committee. It would be even better if from the Worshipful Master down to the Junior Deacon serves on the committee because that is the lodge progressive line. Ideally, the Why, What, and How developed will follow each of those officers into the East. There may be a tweak here and there, but the foundation and framework would remain the same.

While there may be similarities from one Masonic Lodge to the next, the Golden Circle should be developed by incorporating the uniqueness of the members and community that surround the organization. Grand Lodges may have a comprehensive Golden Circle because they support all of the lodges within their jurisdiction. Individual lodges should be more defined and focused based on the interest of their membership and the work that they do within the community. Specialty lodges, like The Harvard Lodge, Texas Lodge of Research, and Tranquility Lodge #2000, all have a particular common interest and will have an even narrower focus than typical Blue Lodges.

Possible Grand Lodge Golden Circle

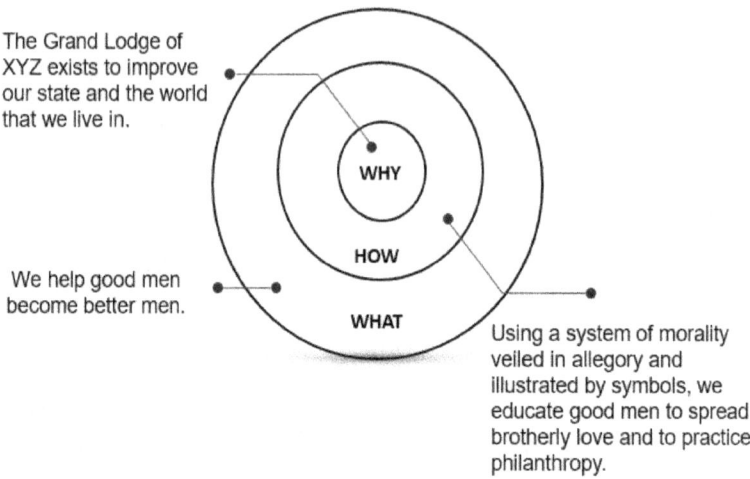

Figure 2: Simon Sinek's Golden Circle Adapted for a Grand Lodge

Possible Blue Lodge Golden Circle

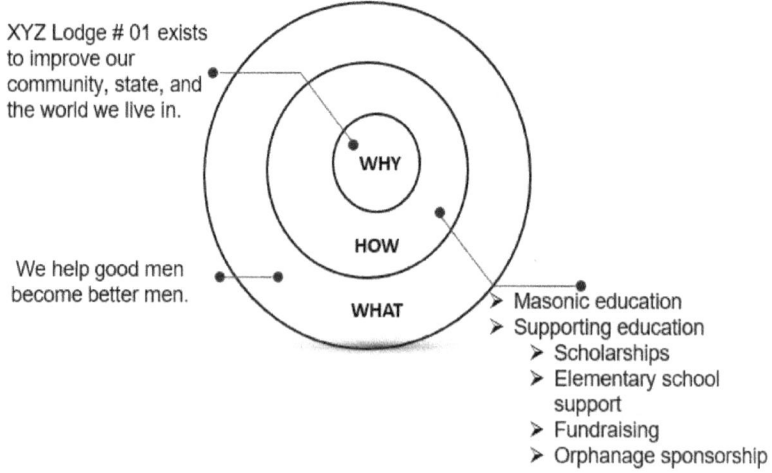

Figure 3: Simon Sinek's Golden Circle Adapted for a Lodge

The process in which the committee develops its strategic plan is not as critical as it is to ensure the stakeholders support the final product. Fundamentally, the Golden Circle is a simple tool for the committee to use. Once the Why, How, and What have been determined, then the committee can begin to define further the lodge's Vision, Mission, and Goals, which will become the blueprint for the work that will be carried on by the officers.

Always Start With Why

Inevitably, after completing the strategic planning process, there will be a need to implement change. Change is not an easy process in Freemasonry. It is essential to build support for change by explaining the Why before any recommendation is made to the members. Sinek pointed out that the human brain processes decision-making based on feelings, not language.[12] Therefore, communicating the reason change is necessary will guide the members of the lodge to be able to rationalize the request for change if they already have a foundational knowledge of the need to change. Examples of how my lodge was able to build the Why first are provided in the next chapter.

Chapter 4

Organization Goals

"Our goals can only be reached through a vehicle of a plan, in which we must fervently believe, and upon which we must vigorously act. There is no other route to success."

- Pablo Picasso.

After the committee has determined the overarching purpose for the Lodge, then it is time to draw the roadmap. Each Masonic organization should have goals or objectives that the officers and members will use to guide them. Goals should be revisited yearly and updated if there are changes or if goals are met.

Valley-Hi Lodge #1407 Goals

For the 2019–2020 Masonic year, as Valley-Hi Lodge #1407 elected officers, we met before the installation to solidify the year's lodge goals. The officers-elect that participated were the Junior Deacon, Senior Deacon, Junior Warden, Senior Warden, and Worshipful Master. The purpose of the first meeting was to set into motion the goals for the entire year. Including all of the line of elected officers in the planning process ensured that the foundation of the planning would have a strong chance of continuing for the next three to five years. Research supports that it takes a minimum of three years to instill lasting change within an organization.

The following meeting minutes serve as an example of how the initial planning meeting and process may run. Each Masonic Lodge is unique and may have a different outcome based upon the Why, membership, and community needs, or resources available.

Visit www.PerfectAshlarPublishing.com to download free resources that are included with the purchase of this book.

Valley-Hi Lodge #1407 Officers-Elect Meeting

June 23, 2019

Establishing the Why, How, & What	Valley-Hi Officers-Elect - Discussed the need to have an established Why. • **Why** = Improvement of the community as a whole. • **How** = Education as a focus. • **What** = Help good men become better men.
Developed Three Goals for 2019–2020	1. **Lodge Sustainability** a. This goal will address items like dues, membership increases, and membership retention. 2. **Facilities updates** a. This goal will address lodge improvements and maintenance. 3. **Education** a. This goal will address esoteric work, Masonic Education in the lodge, and having our philanthropy support for educational organizations.

Committees to Establish	★ Audit Committee ★ Building/Food Committee ★ Education Committee ★ Fundraising Committee ★ Membership Committee
Stated Meeting Length	**SW Elect** - proposed shortening the stated meeting time. **WM Elect** - proposed instituting a 3-minute time limit for members to speak during discussion. After 3 minutes, the member will yield the floor to a Brother and may speak again after another brother speaks. He proposed tabling conversations that were not progressing during stated meeting discussions. **All Officers-Elect** - agreed to implement these new lodge procedures.

Figure 4: Valley-Hi Lodge Officer Meeting Agenda and Minutes

CHAPTER 4

GOAL #1, LODGE SUSTAINABILITY

"There is no doubt in my mind that Masonry is the cornerstone of America."

– Bro. Dave Thomas.

When discussing the Why and goals for Valley-Hi Lodge, the officers-elect reviewed the documents that were used with the most recent audit. It is strongly recommended that the Senior Warden serves on the audit committee to ensure that he has a clear understanding of the state of the organization before beginning his year as the organization's leader. After reviewing the documents and some discussion, the officers felt that before the lodge could set goals that would lead to the membership becoming better men, they had to ensure that the organization would be around for another fifty years.

Dues and Degree Fees

The financial health of a Masonic lodge could be the determining factor for it to remain open or close its doors forever. A quick review of Masonic social media groups and undoubtedly, you will find a post referencing the need to raise dues and then an extensive thread of attached comments on this hot topic. Valley-Hi Lodge is no different from the average Masonic organization. The majority of members are older in age, and most would say they are on a fixed budget. Additionally, several members belong to other appendant bodies, or they have plural memberships with multiple lodges. Therefore, the members are concerned when the topic of raising dues comes up year after year.

Typically, a lodge will set the lodge dues and degree fees and not revisit them for several years. The members forget to consider the rate of inflation. While the utilities, resources, and rent costs continue to increase, the organization's degree fees and yearly dues remain the same. The purchasing power slowly decreases with each passing year, and the organization's savings dwindles. This has a drastic impact on lodge facilities (See more details under Goal 2). Once it becomes evident that something must be done about the organization's finances, the membership needs to act before it's too late.

When the time comes to raise dues, it is critical that the membership understands the Why behind the decision. After being installed Worshipful Master, I mailed a "State of the Lodge" letter to all members. The letter was front and back. It included the three goals developed by the newly installed officers, invited all members to the next meeting to receive a detailed presentation on the lodge finances, and gave a brief history of the lodge dues and how those dues compared to the current day monetary value. This was calculated by using a free online inflation calculator.

The intent of the letter was to inform members, hoping that they would be led to the conclusion that dues and fees needed to increase. We were building the Why without explicitly putting members on the defensive. The Brethren were provided with the lodge's current dues of $100, which was raised 17 years earlier in 2002 with an inflation value for 2019 of $142.28. Also included was the dues from when Valley-Hi Lodge opened in 1964, which was $32 and with a 2019 inflation value equaling $264.41. The information also included the total Lodge revenue and expenses, which showed that the Lodge was in the negative - $1,217.50 every year. What was not included in the total were degree fees, fundraising, and any costs that were accrued from repairs or emergencies. These items were excluded because they were not guaranteed each year. A reproduction of the letter showing a financial breakdown to members is included on the following page.

Current Dues $100		
Date Implemented	Amount	U.S. Calculator Adjustment for Inflation Equivalent to 2019
1964	$32	$264.41
2002	$100	$142.38

Valley-Hi Membership	
Total Valley-Hi Members	117
Dues-Paying Members	62
Endowed Members (Non-Dues-Paying)	51
Life Members (Non-Dues-Paying)	5
50-Year Members	9

Revenue	
62 Members X $100	+ $6,200
Grand Lodge Per Capita $27.50 X 117	- $3,217.50
Total Revenue for Operating Cost	+ $2,982.50
Building Insurance Cost	- $2,000
Utilities (Water, Electricity)	- $2,200
Final Operating Funds	- $1,217.50

Brethren, in an effort to be transparent, we have provided you with the numbers above. The numbers do not include fundraising or degree fees because those are not guaranteed sources of revenue. Due to the generosity of our brothers, degree fees, and fundraising, we do have approximately **$26,810.84** in assets. At this moment, we are not in jeopardy of closing our doors. However, as we continue to maintain our lodge, that fund decreases. Our lodge is at a crossroads, and we need to choose the correct path to secure Valley-HI's legacy in the fraternity. We do continue to have an interest in our lodge and anticipate this to increase.

We will be raising another brother in August. We have 2 active FCs and 2 new EAs. We will keep you posted on the events and decisions of your lodge. **If you are able to do so, please consider making an additional donation to your lodge to use for improvements when you return the updated contact card in the addressed and stamped envelope.**

Figure 5: 2019 Valley-Hi State of the Lodge Letter

There was an overwhelmingly positive response to the letter. Accompanying the letter was a self-addressed stamped envelope to return a contact card so that our lodge could update the records. On that card, there was an option to include a donation to Valley-Hi Lodge. Several of the non-dues-paying members made a monetary donation. The mailout was well worth the $200 cost incurred by our lodge. Not only was the lodge able to update the contact list, but returned envelopes trickled in all summer, resulting in just under $4,000 in donations from our members. Many of the donations came from the endowed members. A copy of the return contact card is included below.

Updated Contact Info

Name _____

Phone _____

Please mail this card back to Valley-Hi to ensure that we can keep you updated with lodge news.

Email _____

Address _____

I have enclosed a $_____ donation to help with lodge repairs and updates.

Figure 6: 2019 Valley-Hi Lodge Updated Contact Info Card

The Valley-Hi State of the Lodge letter invited members to attend the August stated meeting; "At the August 13th stated meeting, Brother Bill Boyd P.M., will be presenting our lodge's current financial health. We will be discussing options for ensuring our financial sustainability for the future."

Brother Boyd is a Valley-Hi Past Master who served in the East in 2015-2016. In his year, he noticed that our lodge was quickly approaching a point that the dues-exempt members would soon surpass the dues-paying members. Brother Boyd spent a significant amount of time gathering the resources necessary to sound the alarm that Valley-Hi Lodge would need to face the possibility of reaching the point of no return. He was aware that dues and degree fees needed to be raised, but it was not until my year as Worshipful Master that we could get enough support to make that change. After the State of the Lodge letter began to establish the Why and opened the door for conversation, the next step was a presentation to allow members an opportunity to consider a vote. Brother Boyd volunteered to prepare and present several scenarios to the lodge members that would ensure lodge financial sustainability.

The following slides presented to members outlined Valley-Hi Lodge's current financial state and the options to be voted on at the next stated meeting.

The Process

Step One – Compute Dues Income According to Member Status

Step Two – Compute Additional Income Sources (estimated)

Step Three - Subtract Expenses (estimated)

Step Four – Options

All three steps are computed for four increments of increases in two separate Per Capita Scenarios

i.e. dues increments at $125, $150, $175, and $200

Current – Dues $100.00 & PER CAPITA $27.50

117 members, 9 are 50-year + members, 5 are Life Members, 51 are Endowed

---

62 dues payers @ $100 each = $6,200

---

62 dues payers + 5 Life Members + 51 Endowed Members @ $27.50 = $3,217.50

$6,200 - $3,217.50 = *$2,982.50*
  Dues   Per capita

$2,982.50 Net Income after per capita

SCENARIO 1 – PER CAPITA REMAINS $27.50

117 members, 9 are 50-year + members, 5 are Life Members, 51 are Endowed

----

62 dues payers @ $125 each = $7,750

----

62 dues payers + 5 Life Members + 51 Endowed Members @ $27.50 = $3,217.50

$7,750 - $3,217.50 = $4,532.50
 Dues   Per capita

$4,532.50 Net Income after per capita

SCENARIO 1 – PER CAPITA REMAINS $27.50

117 members, 9 are 50-year + members, 5 are Life Members, 51 are Endowed

----

62 dues payers @ $150 each = $9,300

----

62 dues payers + 5 Life Members + 51 Endowed Members @ $27.50 = $3,217.50

$9,300 - $3,217.50 = $6,082.50
 Dues   Per capita

$6,082.50 Net Income after per capita

SCENARIO 2 – PER CAPITA INCREASE TO $30.00

117 members, 9 are 50-year + members, 5 are Life Members, 51 are Endowed

----

62 dues payers @ $175 each = $10,850

----

62 dues payers + 5 Life Members + 51 Endowed Members @ $30.00 = $3,510

$10,850 - $3,510 = $7,340
   Dues   Per capita

$7,340 Net Income after per capita

SCENARIO 1 – PER CAPITA REMAINS $27.50

117 members, 9 are 50-year + members, 5 are Life Members, 51 are Endowed

----

62 dues payers @ $200 each = $12,400

----

62 dues payers + 5 Life Members + 51 Endowed Members @ $27.50 = $3,217.50

$12,400 - $3,217.50 = $9,182.50
   Dues   Per capita

$9,182.50 Net Income after per capita

During the final analysis stages, the officers met to iron out the best and worst-case scenarios resulting from member voting on several different options. We wanted to anticipate the members' questions and be prepared for informed discussions about each of the opportunities presented for a vote. By identifying these options in advance, we (the officers) were, in fact, able to provide and discuss all possible scenarios with the members to consider in their deliberations as the voting approached and avoided having the recommendation killed before it was brought to a vote.

Additionally, the officers identified that a reasonable proposal for each degree fee would be $150 per degree. This was a change from the Entered Apprentice degree fee of $125, Fellowcraft degree fee of $75, and the Master Mason degree remained the same at $150. The recommendation to change the degree fees was presented to the membership. After the presentation, the attendees were advised to consider the options and keep in mind that when Valley-Hi Lodge opened in 1964, membership dues were equivalent to approximately $265. There were very few questions and no significant concerns. Next, the lodge sent all the members an electronic copy of the presentation and announced that at the next stated meeting, the Lodge would be voting on raising the degree fees and yearly Lodge dues.

At the following stated meeting, Valley-Hi Lodge voted unanimously to raise yearly dues and all degree fees to $150.

Final Thought on Raising Dues and Degree Fees

Raising dues and degree fees for any organization will be a challenge. The Valley-Hi Lodge example is intended to provide readers with one possible option. Each lodge and membership body is different, so any approach should take the organizational needs and audience into consideration. If it is necessary to address organizational financial sustainability, there are some strategic elements to consider and take the time to build and present a case to all the members. Begin with the formal and informal leaders who will be able to support the recommendation or kill it before it reaches a vote. Start with Why it is necessary to raise fees first, present the rate of inflation, comparing fees from the past, show the value to the members, give a transparent financial report, share how the newly acquired funds will be spent, and finally, request a call to action.

"Any organization that is cheap to join and belong to requires little sense of commitment, pride, or belonging from its members. Any organization that is easy to join is also easy to walk away from."[13] Taking financial needs off the table, is it possible that by raising fees, the fraternity would see an increase in loyal members? In the early 1900s, for many lodges, the cost to join Freemasonry was, on average, equivalent to two weeks' worth of salary.[14] Additionally, on average, each Master Mason contributed, to today's monetary value, the equivalent of nearly $3,000 a year.[15] One of the common questions a prospective member asks is, "How much will it cost?" When told $150, the prospect is almost always shocked to find out that it is per year and not per month. Many Masons leave the Blue Lodge because they are not getting out of the Craft what they expected. Possibly higher fees would lead to more commitment from the members to participate or funds for the organization to have more social activities, charitable events, or education.

It is critical that when fees are raised, the organization adds value to the membership by ensuring that there is a solid return on a member's investment.

Endowments to Sustain a Lodge

Spend a few minutes exploring a Masonic social media group's archived threads, and there will be at least one extensive post with a fiery debate on endowments. Endowments allow members to contribute a multiplied amount of their yearly dues to be invested by the Grand Lodge, which will, in turn, take a portion of the return on that investment and send it back to the lodge each year. The benefit to the Mason is that he is now forever exempt from paying dues. The lodge's benefit is that the Mason's contribution will help the lodge as long as the doors remain open, even after the Brother has laid down his working tools.

It sounds like a win for both parties, so where is the controversy? Depending on the lodge's minimum endowment amount and the return on investment that year will determine the amount an endowment check will be for a lodge. In Texas, the minimum endowment is 5 units at $100 apiece, equal to $500. In a perfect year, an endowment will have a net return of 5%, and $25 would be sent to the lodge.

In 2020, the Grand Lodge of Texas required lodges to pay a per capita of $27.50 per member. A minimum endowment in a perfect year still does not cover the per capita for the endowed Brother leaving the lodge short. However, when the lodge is no longer required to pay a per capita on that same Brother, this is a win for the lodge. Endowments can be a bonus for any lodge, as long as the living members remain active and contribute each year to the lodge financially by donating an amount equal to the current dues or helping to fundraise.

One of my earliest memories at Valley-Hi Lodge was a debate about endowments that occurred in early 2015. The first endowment purchased at the lodge was in 1986 for $500, and the last endowment purchased for $500 was in 2011. By 2011, eighty-six members purchased an endowment for the lodge, and only two of the eighty-six purchased more than the minimum of $500. Between 2011 and 2015, the lodge voted to raise the minimum endowment purchase from 5 units to 10 units, equaling $1,000. By the time the lodge was having a debate about increasing the endowment fee again, no members had purchased an endowment at the new rate of $1,000. The argument was that the endowment minimum should be set at 20 units, equaling $2,000. The idea was that if the endowment were to produce a 5% return on $2,000, then Valley-Hi Lodge would receive $100, which at the time was equivalent to one year of dues. This appealed to the Brothers because very few of the members with $500 endowments were active and donating funds to the lodge. Therefore, the dispute was that their initial $500 investment did not cover the $27.50 per capita required by the Grand Lodge of Texas. That night, the members in attendance voted to raise the minimum endowment from $1,000 to $2,000. Since that vote between 2015 and 2020, only three Brothers have purchased an endowment for $2,000.

In an effort to help the lodge increase its return in endowments, the 2011 change may have hindered its progress by making the minimum investment too high for most members at $1,000. Before the initial 2011 change, Valley-Hi Lodge averaged nearly four endowments per year. In nine years from 2011 to 2020, only three endowments equaling $6,000 were purchased by the members. What if Valley-Hi would have left the endowment at $500, and the average of four new endowments purchased remained steady during those nine years. That could have possibly been thirty-six new endowments equaling $18,000 instead of three at $6,000.

Endowments are risky for a lodge, and they are not a sure thing. The total endowment investment in 2019 for Valley-Hi Lodge was $49,300. That year, the endowment investment return check from the Grand Lodge of Texas was high enough to cover all but $60 of the Valley-Hi Lodge's per capita fee for all its members. The following year in 2020, the market took an enormous hit from the COVID19 pandemic, and the Grand Lodge of Texas endowment investment return check was half of what it was the previous year. However, there were 89 members with endowments, 24 members ($12,000 worth) who were deceased or no longer lodge members. Those 24 Brothers' investments were very beneficial to Valley-Hi Lodge in both 2019 and 2020.

Clearly, there is a strong argument for both sides of the endowment debate. Valley-Hi Lodge saw the benefit of endowments in 2019 when all but $60 of the Grand Lodge of Texas per capita requirement was covered. Lodge sustainability being the number one goal, the officers in 2020 decided to ask the members to commit to at least one fundraiser a year to increase the endowment fund. A motion was put on the floor to host a yearly fundraiser that would raise money to purchase a $500 memorial endowment for a deceased worthy Brother. The first fundraiser was selling 100 commemorative coins to celebrate Valley-Hi Lodge's 50 years in the Valley-Hi community. The lodge officers donated the $400 required to buy the coins. Each coin was sold for $20, each resulting in $2,000 to purchase $500 endowments for four worthy Brothers who the lodge did not have to pay the per capita requirement. The lodge officer discovered a way to honor the Brothers of the past while at the same time securing Valley-Hi Lodge's financial future.

Figure 7: 2020 Valley-Hi Lodge's 50-Year Commemorative Coin – Designed by Bro. Chris King

Organization Procedures and Rules

Once fees are changed, the organization will need to add those changes to the procedures and rules. The procedures and rules act as a governing document for the organization. The procedures and rules document should be revisited each year. Valley-Hi Lodge discovered that it had been over ten years since the procedures and rules had last been updated. The lodge rules committee conducted a full review of the document and realized that some pieces needed to be addressed that were in conflict with recent Grand Lodge rule changes.

Additionally, the committee added a section regarding lodge committee definitions and responsibilities, officer roles and responsibilities, and dress code information.

Organizational sustainability can be impacted by the procedures and rules, or the lack of content within that document can be a viable threat. Valley-Hi Lodge committee members discovered that there was a lack of checks and balances within the text to address the reimbursement of funds for items purchased by various officers. The committee recommended adding additional lodge officers to review any warrants and receipts prior to the disbursement of funds. This addition prevents an accounting error by the secretary or treasurer. While the committee added some additional safeguards, they also added emergency contingencies for the Worshipful Master in case there is a lodge emergency that requires funds to be spent before the next stated meeting.

Membership Recruiting

If there is a term that will quickly get a seasoned Mason's attention, it is "membership recruiting." Most veteran Masons may frown upon the need to recruit and, at the same time, reference a Grand Lodge Law that forbids Blue Lodges from actively recruiting new members. They might even reference a familiar line that pertains to a candidate's free will and accord. That same veteran Mason will hand a brochure from a Masonic appendant body to a newly raised Master Mason. While the term membership recruiting creates a stir among the Brethren, the term "Freemasonry is Dying"[16] should ignite a sense of urgency like a shockwave across our fraternity.

Brother Lance Kennedy did create quite a debate when in his 2018 paper, he concluded that Freemasonry was experiencing a slow death. His data analysis of the Masonic Service Association of North America (MSANA) reported that in North America, an average of 50,000 Masons leaves the fraternity each year. At the height of Freemasonry in 1959, our membership was over 4.1 million, and by 2017, our fraternity was at 1,076,626.[17] Considering these statistics, Freemasonry may already have numbers below 1 million by the time this book is published.

The marketing campaign "**Ask 1 2 B 1**" was a unique way for Freemasons to get the message out that if someone wants to join the fraternity, then they must ask a Mason to become a Mason. This motto is on bumper stickers, car emblems, lodge marques, and websites. There is just one problem with that campaign; whoever sees that motto must know where to find a Mason to ask them to become one. Chance is that in the 21st century, a stranger is less likely to approach a stranger on the street, and driving 75 mph on a highway is not conducive to pulling up next to a vehicle and yelling to the driver, "How do I become a Mason?" Therefore, the lodge must create these opportunities for potential prospects.

Lodge Events

The tried-and-true open house is always a favorite event for lodges to host. Some jurisdictions require them. Our lodge discovered that anytime we had an open house, it was just another event where we could come together as a lodge with maybe one or two prospects that one of our Brothers would drag along with him. We needed some way to increase the lodge traffic, so we paired our open house with a Trunk-or-Treat on Halloween. Lodge Brothers donated the candy, we advertised to the neighborhood that Valley-Hi Lodge provided a safe place for trick-or-treating, and the lodge would be open to visitors.

We handed out a lot of candy and had some great discussions with moms and dads in the parking lot. We posted some pictures and received several thank-yous from the neighborhood. One online commentary was happy that we were getting involved in the community. It was a win-win because we successfully had an open house, were visible in the community, and gave back by providing a safe place for kids to trick-or-treat.

Figure 8: 2018 Valley-Hi Lodge's Trunk or Treat Facebook Post

Figure 9: 2018 Valley-Hi Lodge's Trunk or Treat Flyer Posted to Facebook & Nextdoor App

Lodges need to be very creative while planning their events. Lodge members should consider how an event can engage the community and raise the profile of the lodge. Here are a few key things to keep in mind when planning events that will attract potential members:

1. What is in it for the visitor? People will come if there is something in it for them. Fundraisers are great, but those are primarily for the lodge. Try to keep it FREE for the visitors.
2. Advertise! There are some inexpensive ways to advertise.
3. Get the Brothers to help with the event and bring guests.
4. Take lots of pictures during the event.
5. Post a summary of the event and photos on your webpage and on social media.

Social Media

The importance of social media to find new members cannot be understated. One of my biggest frustrations as Worshipful Master was the inability to find among the aging members those who are able-bodied and healthy enough to contribute to our lodge's operations. One way to solve this problem is to attract younger members. In 2018, Brother Steve McCall shared some sobering facts about the adults between the ages of 18 to 29:

- They spend 1.8 hours on social media per day.
- 81% have a Facebook profile.
- 46% have an Instagram account.
- 38% have a Twitter account.
- 36% have a Snapchat account.[18]

Brother McCall stressed the importance that social media has for millennials to obtain their news and information. My children, Gabriella, 19, and Thomas, 15, are considered Generation Z, and they rely on YouTube and TikTok for their entertainment and to acquire information. The future of any lodge will be dictated by its social media footprint.

Figure 10: Valley-Hi Lodge's 2020 Facebook Page Cover Photo

Having a presence on social media does not have to be overly complicated. Start small with creating a Facebook account. As Brother McCall reported, Facebook will yield the greatest return on your effort based on the numbers. First, as a Worshipful Master, find a younger member familiar with social media to create a Facebook page for the lodge. If the lodge doesn't have one, ask a friend or family member to set up a free page. Facebook pages are open to the public and easy to maintain. The lodge can post pictures, information, create ads, and schedule events.

Additionally, visitors to your page can send messages to the page administrators. Have more than one Facebook page administrator, and do not put it all on your lodge secretary. The secretary can be an administrator, but he is entirely too busy to keep up with a Facebook page full-time. There needs to be consistent activity from the lodge on the page, and messages from visitors need to be returned in a timely manner. Post pictures of the lodge and membership activities, memes on holidays, and Masonic education that is appropriate for the public. Valley-Hi Lodge is very active on our Facebook page, with over 1,300 people who like and follow the page. Administrators for the page can view and track the analytics (activity) on the Facebook page. Here is an example of October 2020:

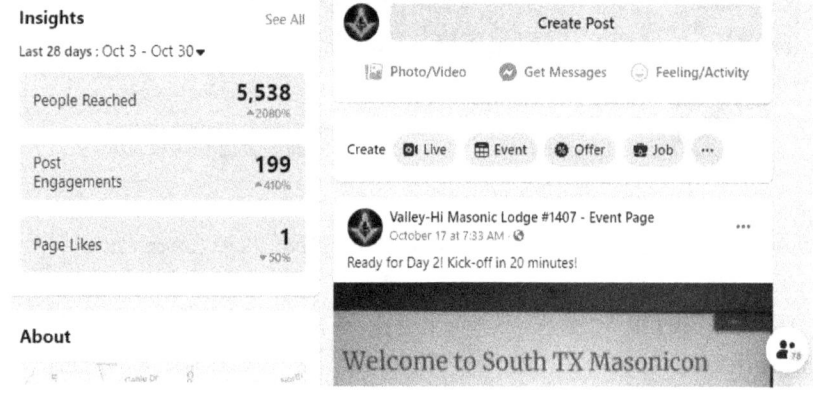

Figure 11: Valley-Hi Lodge's Facebook Analytics for October 2020

Valley-Hi Lodge receives, on average, two prospects a month from their Facebook page. In the Fall of 2019, we had two Master Masons join the lodge after moving to Texas from other states. This was a massive win for the lodge because these were Master Masons who were qualified to become immediate dues-paying members. When asked why they reached out and decided to join Valley-Hi Lodge, both responded because they found the lodge's Facebook page and liked that the membership was so active. In reality, Valley-Hi Lodge is not more active than any other Masonic lodge, but the frequent posts on the page communicated a message that we are engaged in the community and focused on Masonic education.

Facebook has a feature called Facebook Ads. If a lodge has the means, this is an excellent way to target Facebook users within 5 to 10 miles of the lodge. The lodge can create an ad for an event or promote its activities by "Boosting" a post. After a page administrator identifies a post or creates an ad, they can set the target area (e.g., zip code or geographic location on a map) and target demographic (e.g., Males, 18-65 with incomes above $25k). The administrator will then set a cost limit (e.g., $5 per day up to a total of $35) and a time limit the ad will run (e.g., 7 days).

Based on the provided examples, once posted, any male from 18 to 65 years old with an income of $25k a year on Facebook within an identified zip code will see the lodge's ad or post. If they click on it, Facebook will charge the lodge until they reach $5 each day. If the ad is scheduled to run for seven days, it will run until the time is up or the lodge meets its minimum ad spend. For more information on Facebook ads, The Masonic Roundtable Podcast highlighted social media marketing on episode 277.[19]

Facebook ads cost money; therefore, it may not be feasible for every Lodge. Another social media platform not frequently discussed is the Nextdoor App. The Nextdoor App is similar to Facebook but has a very targeted reach. Instead of adding friends to view posts, users are networked with their neighbors. I became aware of the Nextdoor App as an elementary school principal. There were rumors that parents were saying negative things about the school that I supervised. After signing up for an account on the Nextdoor App, I responded to negative posts as the campus principal. This began a positive marketing campaign that would change the neighborhood's perception of the school. The best part is the Nextdoor App is FREE and can target all the communities around a lodge's location. Valley-Hi Lodge's posts can be seen by over 10,000 users within a small radius of the lodge.

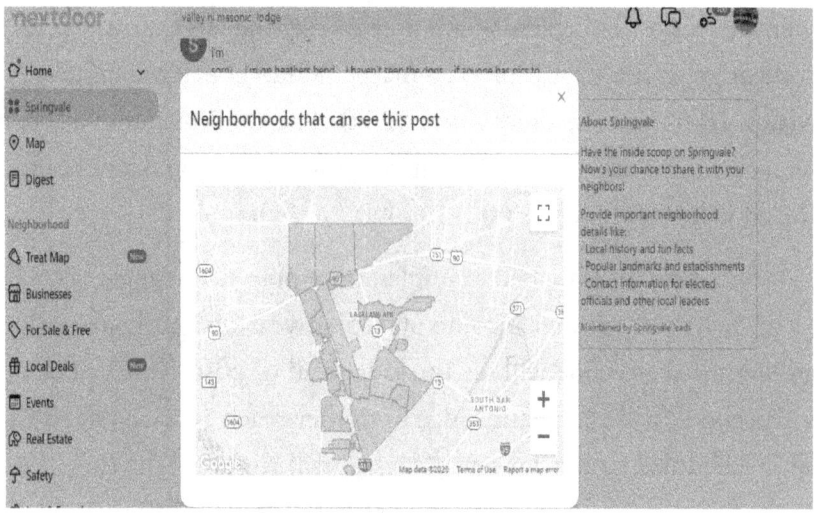

Figure 12: Nextdoor App with the highlighted Neighborhoods Around Valley-Hi Lodge

The Nextdoor App truly is a game-changer for community organizations like Masonic lodges. With this App, Valley-Hi Lodge can engage the community every time they help the local school, host an event, fundraise, or send out information about the lodge. Additionally, the Nextdoor App is a quick way to get a pulse on the community, learn about criminal activity in the area, or find families in need of support from the lodge, all of this at no financial cost to the lodge. There is one drawback. Technically, only one person can hold an account at a time, and the profile must be in a person's name and not the lodge's name. Here is how Valley-Hi Lodge has their profile set up:

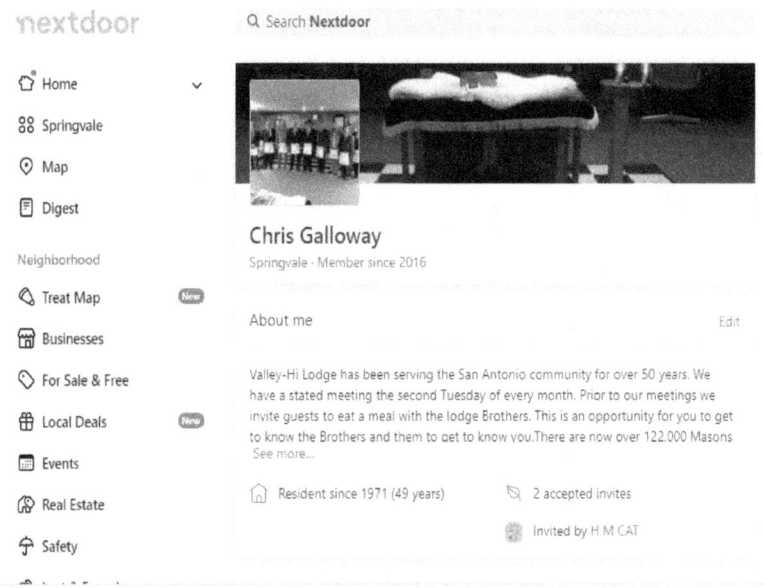

Figure 13: Valley-Hi Lodge's Nextdoor App Profile Page

Figure 14: Valley-Hi Lodge Nextdoor App Post, September 11, 2020

Lodge History

Up to this point, the focus of Goal #1 has been on keeping the lodge doors open. The mystique of a lodge is rooted in its history. Therefore, history must be preserved and showcased to the members and the curious. When a prospect knocks on the lodge door, imagine the impact of a guide sharing with him the amazing history of the lodge as they walk by the pictures of the Past Masters who have guided the lodge before him. As the lodge ages, the binders of minutes will grow taller, and the stories will become richer. Unfortunately, too many lodges have had their history wiped out in an instance by a fire, flood, or tornado.

Lodge members can learn so much by taking a deep dive into the minutes of their lodge. For example, after reading the 1964 to 1970 minutes of Valley-Hi Lodge, I discovered that the lodge rented space from another local lodge while they searched for a permanent home. Several options fell through until a well-respected San

Antonio, Texas builder donated some land and offered to build the lodge building at a cost. The original charter members donated the $13,000 to construct the building so that the lodge would have no debt when they moved into their new lodge on November 3, 1970. This is valuable information that I shared with the members of Valley-Hi in 2018 when the lodge officers discussed the need to refurbish the facilities to prevent the building from degrading. Once again, establishing the "Why" before asking the members to vote on an item required to spend saved funds.

While sitting in the East, Worshipful Masters are responsible for guarding the Charter and the lodge as a whole. "You now receive in charge the Charter, by the authority of which this lodge is held. You are carefully to preserve and duly transmit it to your successor in office."[20] Consider the following questions as you reflect on the previous statement read to the Worshipful Master during his installation: Is the Charter hanging on the wall in a fireproof frame? Or is the Charter on the wall a copy with the original safely stored in a fireproof safe? Are all the lodge records and minutes in a fireproof area safe from insects or water? If the answer is no, then it may be time to get to work. Depending on the lodge's age, this could be an extensive project that will require multiple people, but once it is complete, then any Worshipful Master that follows needs only to maintain the progress made. Listen to The Masonic Round Table Podcast to learn more about the Lodge history preservation process and historian position.[21]

A prudent Worshipful Master will always consult his Grand Lodge Law Book before beginning any project of this magnitude. In a good-faith effort, there is the potential for a lodge to make a mistake and break a Grand Lodge law while establishing a new practice. For example, the Grand Lodge of Texas does not allow a Blue Lodge officer position to be officially designated as a historian; however, the Worshipful Master may establish a Lodge History Committee to oversee a project to preserve the lodge history. Some Grand Lodge's may frown upon electronically filing minutes or have specific guidelines on safeguarding these files. There are several considerations on how to tackle documenting the history of your lodge. As Worshipful Master, you can never be too cautious, so take the time to ensure that someone researches what is allowable by your state Grand Lodge. The following is an adapted outline of Brother William H. Boyd's 2020[22] white paper on duties and responsibilities for an established Lodge History Committee:

- Create an overall Lodge Filing Plan to account for and organize all lodge documentation and historical records (minutes, correspondence, documents, charters, photos, communications, etc.).
- Capture and electronically file/organize lodge meeting minutes. Once the historical minutes have been electronically filed and organized under the Filing Plan, the History Committee should concentrate on electronically preserving and filing each Masonic year's minutes. So, as not to intrude on the Secretary's duties, at the beginning of each new masonic year, the History Committee will begin electronically capturing the previous year's minutes and filing them according to the Filing Plan. **Keep these files protected on multiple devices or**

drives to avoid technology issues destroying the committee's work.
- Electronically capture and file/organize images of key lodge documents (charter, UD Warrant, Certificates, Grand Lodge Awards/Certificates, Community Awards/Certificates, Past Master photos, portraits, etc.).
- Conduct and file member interviews on video, stored in accordance with the Lodge Filing Plan (History Committee should develop a standard interview script to ensure some specific information is captured for each member that is interviewed. History Committee should, at a minimum, interview any living Charter Members and Past Masters available for contact).
- Publish the lodge history. The committee's Chairman should coordinate with their Grand Lodge Library or Secretary and plan on delivering a copy of the final document to them when published. The Chairman should publish the initial publication and updates at a defined interval, possibly every ten years, but at least every 25 years.
- Encourage and assist the lodge Brethren in creating Masonic biographies or resumes, documenting their degree dates, offices and installation dates, awards, and so forth. The History Committee should develop a standard format for ease of filing and continuity.
- Maintain the historic lodge files; create a duplicate of the electronic files and filing plan and store offsite.

Update throughout the year with documentation of events, copies of correspondence, records, etc.

In his 2020 paper, Brother Boyd described the History Process[23] as

1. Gather your data and materials.
2. Organize the data and material; create your Filing Plan.
3. Create your electronic archive; save your data and materials to electronic files.
4. Maintain throughout the year as events occur, documents are created or received, etc.
5. Publish your lodge history and then update it at a defined interval.

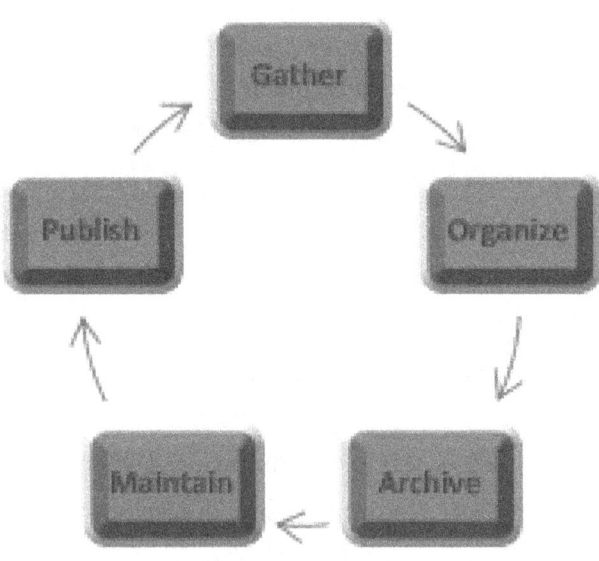

Figure 15: William H. Boyd's 2020 History Process

Chapter 5

Goal #2, Lodge Facilities

"One thing and only one thing a Masonic Lodge can give its members which they can get nowhere else in the world. That one thing is Masonry."

– Bro. Carl H. Claudy.

In 1856, Brother Albert G. Mackey noted that the Old Charges define a lodge to be "a place where Masons assemble and work;" he continued to define a lodge, quoting the lecture from the first degree, which defines that "a lodge is an assemblage of Masons, duly congregated, having the Holy Bible, square, and compasses, and a charter, or warrant of constitution, empowering them to work."[24] Theoretically, a lodge is anywhere that has the items mentioned above present and an appropriate number of Master Masons ready for work. The reality is that without a permanent facility, it would be challenging for prospects and members to know where to go. The lodge must have a place to call its own. For some, this may be a stand-alone building, a room within another facility, or another lodge building that the members rent for meetings and events.

This section will hopefully provide examples and ideas that can be used to improve your lodge. I believe that we learn from our mistakes. Therefore, in the next few pages, there is a certain level of transparency intended to inform the reader and not meant to be critical of my mother lodge. It is vital to share details in their full context so that the reader can make connections to the text and draw parallels to their own lodge experiences. I do not doubt that Valley-Hi Lodge members had the very best intentions with the decisions they made regarding lodge facilities, but we have learned from the mistakes made. I hope that after reading the content that follows, the you will walk away with a good understanding of what did not work for our lodge and how we grew from it to improve our building vastly.

First Impressions

Can you recall the feeling you had the first time you knocked upon the outside of your lodge's door? The mystery that awaited you as you entered into unknown territory. What did you see? What did you hear? What did you smell? Most likely, you were nervous and possibly a little excited. Your first impression of your mother lodge may have sealed the deal for you, but for others, it may have been what prevented them from turning in a petition. The first impression that your lodge portrays is a serious consideration for any current or future Worshipful Master.

As mentioned in the Journey to the East chapter of this book, I was at rock bottom when I knocked upon Valley-Hi Lodge's door, so my need to belong to something bigger than myself overpowered my first impressions of my mother lodge. In 2013, the parking area of Valley-Hi Lodge was a shell of a parking lot taken over by the overgrown vegetation. The entrance to Valley-Hi Lodge opened into a mid-1990's addition to the original 1970's lodge building. The main area was overdue for a paint job, the walls had water stains and damage from a leaky roof, and cracks splintered throughout the ceiling.

This may be a good point to insert a quote from the Journey to the East section regarding the two lodges that I emailed for information, "The other lodge never responded. I am relatively confident that there would have been a good chance that I would have joined the other lodge because it was geographically closer to my apartment," and the facilities at Valley-Hi Lodge did not communicate a warm welcome. Luckily the members in attendance that night were very engaged with me, my story, and with open arms, encouraged me to consider petitioning. There are no regrets with my decision to petition Valley-Hi Lodge; communication was a key component to my recruitment and retention. It cannot be overstated that communication with prospects can be critical or determinantal to your lodge's membership recruitment and sustainability.

Analysis Paralysis

How did we get here? This was a question that could be seen on the faces of many of the members of Valley-Hi Lodge as we sat in another stated meeting, debating how we would act to repair our lodge. The repairs that were required are of no consequence because the result was often the same each month. One of the motivated Brothers would stand and address the Brethren by declaring that something within the lodge needed to be repaired. Another Brother would stand and say that he knows a guy who knows a guy who can do the job that needs to be done. A different Brother would stand and make the statement that he had done similar work on his house and that the cost would be too high. Yet another Brother would then stand and refute the last Brother and say that he also had a similar job done on his house, and the price was significantly lower. Finally, after

30 minutes, the Worshipful Master would stand and form a committee to bring back to the lodge a minimum of three quotes and then drop his gavel, ending the long debate.

The following month, the lodge room would be in anticipation, waiting for the Worshipful Master to open the discussion for "Old Business." The Brothers who were assigned to secure three price quotes would present their findings to the members. The same Brothers who spoke up at the last stated meeting would stand and rehash their opinions on the floor for another 30 minutes. Then the consensus would be that the best course of action would be for a few Brothers to meet on the weekend to complete the repair themselves at a much lower cost to the lodge and with no guarantee or warranty on the work.

This same process occurred month after month. If repairs for an electronic device (e.g., a computer) were not feasible in some situations, a Brother would kindly donate to the lodge a replacement that was no longer needed in their own home. For extensive repairs with high price tags, such as a parking lot, the Brothers would go through a similar process, but the topic would remain unresolved. In business and psychology, the term "analysis paralysis" has been coined for similar situations.[25]

The Riding Lawnmower

Analysis paralysis results from overanalyzing, confusion, or being overwhelmed with having to make a difficult decision.[26] In business, especially the financial business fields, the term is used to describe a customer who is so overwhelmed they make irrational decisions that seem simpler but ultimately lead to disaster.[27] The seasoned members at Valley-Hi Lodge meant well and were trying to be frugal with the lodge funds; however, the patchwork repairs were not lasting and ended up in the long run costing the members more in the end. For example, the lodge's riding lawnmower consistently broke down, and a Brother would buy a part and fix it until one day, even the repair shop could not fix it. The members voted to contract with a lawn mowing service until the lawnmower could be repaired. One year and $1,200 later, the members finally voted to purchase a brand-new riding lawn mower with a 5-year warranty for $1,600.

The Parking Lot

Analysis paralysis from the need to spend money to repair and update the lodge led to patchwork for years at Valley-Hi Lodge. Eventually, even the repairs eroded to the point that the easy fixes were no longer viable. Additionally, not having a professional complete the work left the repairs cosmetically noticeable. This leads back to the discussion regarding first impressions. As mentioned in the opening of this chapter, Valley-Hi Lodge had a parking lot taken over by vegetation.

A few years before my first visit to Valley-Hi Lodge, a charter member who passed away left $25,000 to the lodge to be used to replace the parking lot. However, analysis paralysis from spending that amount of money prevented the Brethren from fulfilling our past Brother's wishes until three years after my arrival. It was building the Why and reinforcing the importance of first impressions that finally led to the vote to repair the parking lot.

The Roof

In addition to a neglected parking area, a leaky roof caused water stains and crumbling drywall inside the building. Like clockwork, in the Springtime, the Brothers would form a weekend work party to apply some form of sealant to patch the roof and skylight windows. Despite these efforts, with each rain, strategically placed trashcans were required to collect the incoming water. One stated meeting night while sitting in the West, and as a member of the building committee, I proposed that the roof needed to be replaced by a professional. The proposal started with the Why by making the same case that first impressions were essential and that the cost to keep patching up the roof would only increase. Additionally, another Brother pointed out that there was a strong possibility that mold was already present from the years of a leaky roof. This time, the Why was not strong enough. There was a significant debate on the floor. The parking lot's recent struggles and high costs were still very fresh in the members' minds. A few Brothers were not very Brotherly during the discussion. Unfortunately, it was that night that we lost three Entered Apprentices. It is difficult to know if two of the Entered Apprentices did not return because of the discussion that night, but one of the three was my father-in-law, and after that night, he did not return, proclaiming, "I didn't sign up for this."

A few compelling lessons were revealed that night. When posing a significant and expensive lodge project, the first lesson was bringing all the information to the floor. Starting with the Why was not enough. The members needed to know the project's cost and timeline before they could make an informed decision.

The second lesson was that there should have been strategic meetings to discuss the possible project options before being discussed in a stated meeting. Officers, Past Masters, and members should have been invited to an information meeting to discuss options and address any concerns. A lesson heeded a year later when it was time to raise the yearly dues. Finally, if possible, do not have Entered Apprentice or Fellow Craft Masons present in a stated meeting that could become contentious.

That night, a decision was not made, and the Worshipful Master allowed for the building committee to explore possible options to bring back to the next stated meeting. The lodge's building insurance company and three roofers were contacted to provide quotes. The insurance company determined that the entire roof needed to be replaced. Valley-Hi Lodge received a check for the total cost to replace the roof minus a $1,000 deductible. The Lodge was able to repair the roof with green tiles that matched the lodge colors and received a full warranty on the work, which only cost $1,000. Unfortunately, the damage was already done with the loss of three Entered Apprentice Masons.

Figure 16: Picture & Google Earth Pictures of Before and After Repairs of the Parking Lot & Roof

A New Approach

Are there situations similar to those described above in your lodge? If so, then it may be time to take a new approach to lodge facilities. The 2019 elected officers of Valley-Hi Lodge and a few recent Past Masters committed to focusing on improving lodge facilities without taking any short cuts. This new approach would mean that whenever possible, the lodge would contract with a professional to complete the work so that there would be a guarantee and warranty attached to each project. A contractor has insurance to protect against loss due to a mistake or negligence, which is lacking when Brothers decide to schedule a work party to repair something with the lodge building. The cost of hiring a contractor was still a concern for the incoming officers, so this new strategy would require them to think outside the box.

Community College Support

In the San Antonio area, there are several community colleges. St. Philips College has a very robust construction program. In the summer of 2019, the newly installed Junior Deacon, Brother Adam Sanchez, contacted a teacher from the St. Philips College construction department to inquire about a partnership to repair and refurbish the Valley-Hi Lodge. The teacher visited the lodge to evaluate what work needed to be done. During his visit, the teacher learned more about what Valley-Hi Lodge and other Masonic organizations do for the community. Moved by the fraternity's community work and mission to help good men become better men, the teacher informed Brother Sanchez that he was also a member of a trade organization called the National Home Builders Association

(NHBA). The group has construction workers, electricians, and plumbers that volunteer their time and skills to help worthy organizations. The teacher offered to nominate Valley-Hi Lodge to receive the support.

In return, the lodge had to provide the supplies and allow the St. Philips College construction students to work alongside the contractors.

This new-found knowledge quickly shifted the conversation from repairing the water damage and ceiling cracks to a full Lodge refurbishment. The teacher began to note any significant repairs, then moved to imperfections, outdated items, and finally, a lodge wishlist. The only work that was off the table was flooring. He noted water damage from the leaky roof in the dining area and bathrooms, outdated lighting and ceiling fans throughout, cracks in the ceiling, outdated toilets and sinks/vanities in three bathrooms, and an old kitchen that needed to be demolished in what is now the secretary's office. The lodge requested to have added to the list a server window installed in a wall between the kitchen and dining area.

The construction teacher left excited about the potential project, and a few days later, emailed Brother Sanchez a list of items that Valley-Hi Lodge needed to purchase for the work to be done. If the Brothers had hired contractors with the supplies and labor necessary to complete all the items on the list, it would have cost them an estimated $20,000 to $30,000. The quote for all the things the NHBA and St. Philips College needed was only $6,000. The teacher nominated Valley-Hi Lodge, and the NHBA agreed to support the work.

It was a win-win for the organization to gain some publicity from helping the lodge, for the construction students to gain experience outside the classroom, and for the Valley-Hi Lodge Brothers to make high-quality improvements to the facilities, at a fraction of the cost. Thinking outside the box and taking a risk led to a considerable reward for Valley-Hi Lodge. Worshipful Masters should consider reaching out to known community organizations to seek partnerships to help their lodge and with any future projects. The worst thing that can happen is the organization says no.

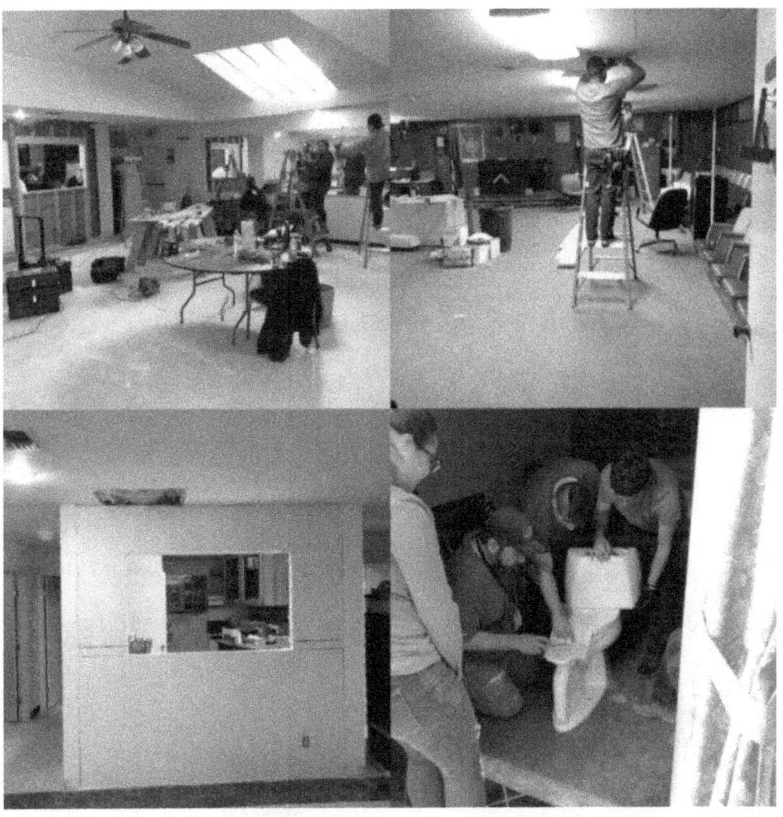

Figure 17: Pictures of the Construction Students Working on Valley-Hi Lodge

Flooring

The NHBA and St. Philips College could not repair or install flooring. Therefore, if the Brothers were to stick to their new approach, they would need to find a contractor. The officers decided to use a website called Angie's List to locate a reputable flooring contractor to install new tiles in the restrooms and place a checkered pavement around the lodge room altar. Angie's List is a website that Valley-Hi Lodge had used in the past to locate an A/C repair company. It is a valuable tool that provides reviews for the consumer, ratings, and contractors to bid for a consumer's business. According to their website,

> Founded in 1995, Angie's List is a leading online ratings and reviews platform that provides trusted reviews and information to help millions of consumers make smart hiring decisions. Angie's List offers more than 15 million verified reviews in over 700 service categories, providing its members with a credible resource for researching and comparing local service providers.[28]

Angie's List is just one free option for lodges to shop for a potential contractor. In smaller towns, it may be easier to reach out to the local Chamber of Commerce. The important thing is that a Worshipful Master should seek all potential options and get the most reputable contractor at an economical price. Valley-Hi Lodge was able to get the flooring work in the three bathrooms and around the altar completed for $700.

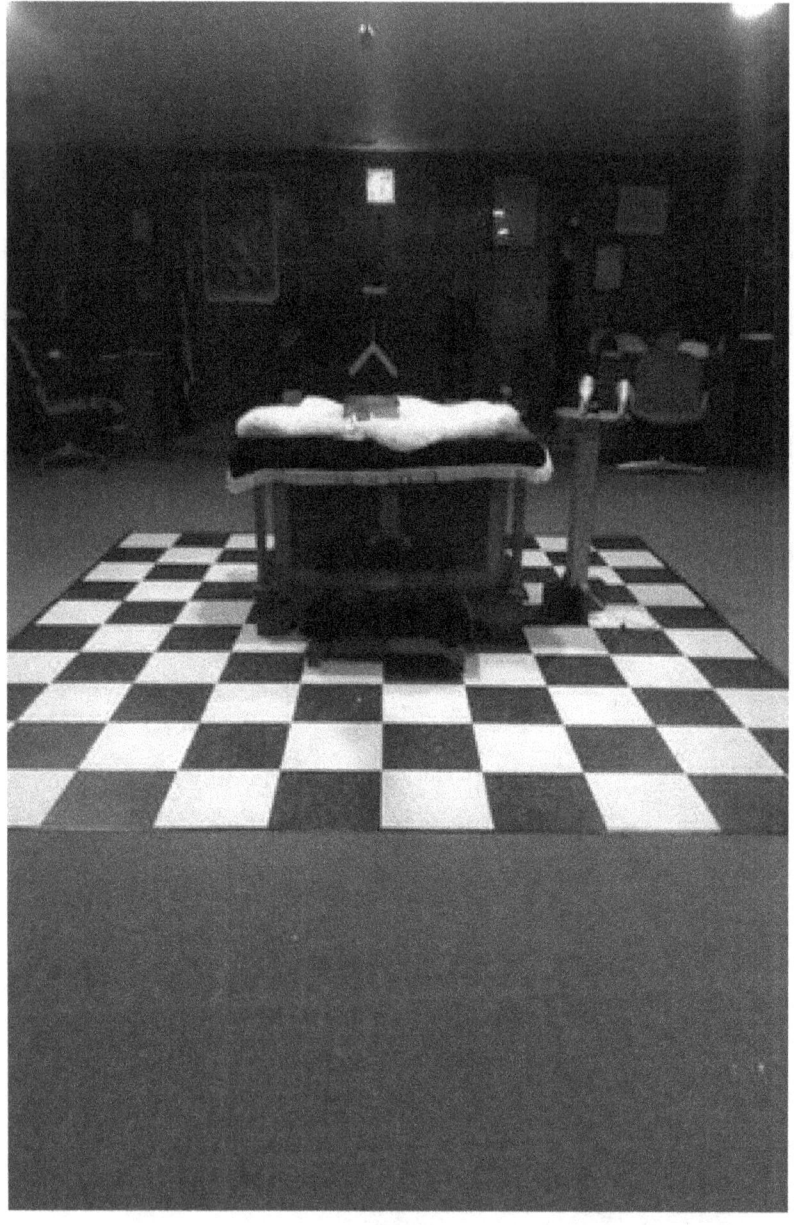

Figure 18: Pictures of the Checkered Pavement Around the Altar

Pitching In

While the 2019 elected officers did commit to a new approach by hiring professional contractors for repair work, it made sense that the Brothers could pitch in to help for some work: painting, cleaning, installing electrical faceplate covers, and any small repairs or installations. Additionally, the COVID19 Pandemic hit, shutting down the Valley-Hi Lodge, St. Philips College, and the refurbishment project. Once it was safe to do so, a few of the Valley-Hi Lodge Brothers got together with Entered Apprentice Masons, family members, and potential prospects to wrap up some of the unfinished community college students' work.

They painted the new bathrooms, lodge waiting area, and the Ante Room. The Ante Room is literally the entrance for a prospect as he enters into Freemasonry. This area should be a place for him to reflect on the journey he is about to embark upon. Some lodges use the Ante Room for storage and as a place to prepare the candidate, which is not conducive to calming or reflective thoughts before they knock on the door of Freemasonry. Valley-Hi Lodge Brothers removed the clutter from their Ante Room, painted the room green to match the lodge colors, added some artwork by Brother Juan Sepulveda to the wall, a mirror, a few wall stickers, and a giant Masonic sword. Once again, first impressions are everything.

The initiation experience should make an impression on a Mason that will remain with him until he lays down his working tools. Another area that needed much work was the exterior of the lodge building. Valley-Hi Lodge is located in a community that historically has been plagued with graffiti. Unfortunately, the lodge building has been, on more than a few occasions, the focal point of local taggers. It did not help that the exterior had giant whiteboards where a window may have been placed if the building was not a Masonic lodge. These were the perfect canvas for the community graffiti artist. Brothers came together to paint the whiteboards dark green to match the new roof. They had a professional power wash on the bricks and then sealed the building's exterior with 5 gallons of Anti-Graffiti Sealant purchased at Home Depot for less than $200. The sealant carried a 3 to 5-year guarantee.

The work that the Brothers and prospects completed on the facilities at Valley-Hi Lodge was not only beneficial to the organization, but it also paid enormous dividends to those involved. Due to the COVID19 Pandemic, the country had just come out of the most massive shutdown in its history. There was definitely a strong sense of accomplishment, pride, comradery, and Brotherly love that was felt by everyone involved. A handful of people worked on the project, but several older members stopped by to see the progress. It was great to see the veteran members beam with pride and reminisce of their youthful days when they rolled up their sleeves to work on the lodge they, too, love so much. At this moment, the Brothers truly understood the real payment bestowed to Freemasons for their work.

Figure 19: Before & After Pictures of the Ante Room

Figure 20: Ante Room Artwork and Wall Stickers

Figure 21: Valley-Hi Lodge Before & After Exterior Work

Chapter 7

Goal #3, Education

"Education is the key to unlock the golden door of freedom."

– Bro. George Washington Carver, 1896.

In an 1896 letter to Brother Booker T. Washington, Brother George Washington Carver proclaimed that education is the key to freedom.[29] The letter was in response to Brother Booker's request for him to work at the now famed African-American Tuskegee Institute where Brother Carver would have the "task of bringing people from degradation, poverty, and waste to full manhood."[30] At the Valley-Hi Lodge, June 2019 officers-elect meeting, the importance of education to the community and its importance to the lodge were discussed. The soon-to-be-installed officers concluded that education would be the focal point for Valley-Hi Lodge's philanthropy and Masonic work. Therefore, education became Goal #3.

Philanthropy

In the previous chapter, it was noted that after a contentious debate at a Valley-Hi Lodge stated meeting about a leaky roof, my father-in-law commented that he "didn't sign up for this." He joined Freemasonry for two reasons, first to be closer to me, and he joined to roll up his sleeves and give back to the community. Philanthropy and giving back are not only crucial to my father-in-law but, according to Masonic author Matt Nelson, an entire generation of

"Millennials are driven by the desire to make a difference."[31] He also warned that "the catch is that they believe they can do it *right now*, and have no time to waste."[32] Lodges that do not tap into their current and future members' desire to give back to the community may lose them to other community organizations. A lodge that is active in the community will fill that need within those Brothers who desire to be charitable. According to the SIRC research study conducted for the UGLE, one Mason reported that "charity is another thing that attracted me to Freemasonry. It is easy to give in Freemasonry because we enjoy ourselves at the same time."[33] Whether it is a fundraising event for scholarships or buying and dropping off school supplies to a school, Brothers working together for a charitable cause strengthen their Brotherly bond.

Additionally, an active lodge is visible in the community. The visibility of Masons doing charitable work paints a positive image for the Blue Lodge and the fraternity. In regards to Freemasons' publicizing their philanthropic activities, one Mason during the SIRC study noted, "The problem with Freemasonry and the bad press, in my opinion, is that nobody tells anybody about it…The Freemasons give far more, but we keep quiet about it."[34] Encourage Brothers who are comfortable to post pictures of their experiences on social media. Ensure that any activity, but most especially philanthropy work, gets posted to the lodge's social media pages. While it is admirable to be humble, aside from current members' family and friends, the best marketing that a lodge can have is the positive exposure within the community.

Today, it would not be easy to find an organization without a social media account. Another opportunity to gain positive exposure, tag the organization that the lodge is supporting in a post. An example of this is in Figure 22. Valley-Hi Lodge gave the local elementary $500 in school supplies. Posting as the Worshipful Master, I shared a picture of the two Past Masters that delivered the supplies and the assistant principal who received them on the Nextdoor App and Twitter. On the Twitter post, we tagged the school's Twitter account (with the Principal's permission). That post was seen by all the parents and any community members who follow the school's Twitter account.

Figure 22: Valley-Hi Lodge Twitter Post

Local Elementary & Orphanage

The Valley-Hi Lodge-elected officers chose to keep the two primary focuses for their charitable work on the elementary that was only a few blocks away and on the nearby orphanage. The lodge already had relationships with both organizations, and they were comfortable with reaching out to the lodge for support. It made sense to keep those partnerships going into the future. Both the school and orphanage have a role in educating; maintaining the relationship with them aligned with Valley-Hi Lodge's third goal.

At the June 2019 officers-elect meeting, the participants discussed the lodge's role in removing barriers to education. Schools face the challenge of educating students who come from broken homes, do not have adequate healthcare, are hungry, have clothes that are dirty or don't fit, lack school supplies, or are homeless, all of which are distractions to a student's learning. Valley-Hi Lodge provides clothes, school supplies, gift cards to the grocery store for families, and the fantastic teeth program to teach students good oral health. There are times when the lodge will receive a specific request. For example, the elementary school had a pumpkin painting fundraiser during their Fall Festival. Valley-Hi Lodge supplied the pumpkins for that event.

Scholarships

Scholarships are an excellent way for a lodge to give back to the community and directly impact students' education. In 2019, Valley-Hi Lodge no longer had a scholarship. The 2019–2020 officers wanted to start a scholarship that would either support a trades student at a community college or send a student from the local elementary school to an educational camp. Several organizations will match funding from a scholarship. In Texas, the Texas Masonic Charities Foundation (TMCF) provides up to $1,000 matching funds to lodges for scholarships. Valley-Hi Lodge applied for funding from TMCF and was approved, increasing the scholarship from $1,000 to $2,000. Valley-Hi Lodge voted to award $500 scholarships to four students from St. Philips College's construction department. Our members wanted to show gratitude to the students and school for the work they had done on the lodge refurbishment.

Unfortunately, the COVID19 pandemic caused lodges to go dark in the Spring, preventing scholarships from being awarded until the following Fall, which is why it is vital to ensure that all the elected officers are on the same page. While the pandemic prevented the scholarships from being awarded in the 2019–2020 year, the 2020–2021 Masonic year's officers kept the same goals from the previous year. Therefore, the education goal remained, and the students received their scholarships.

Masonic Education

As Worshipful Master, you may choose to assign a Brother to lead your lodge's education, but ultimately, it is your responsibility to ensure that it happens. One of Brother Benjamin Franklin's timeless quotes is, "Tell me, and I forget, teach me, and I may remember, involve me, and I learn." The more that the Brethren of the lodge discuss Masonic education and participate in degrees and research outside their Blue Lodge, the more they will learn and grow as Masons. Building capacity is critical because the young Master

Masons in your lodge today will become tomorrow's mentors. When I first joined Valley-Hi Lodge, we had three very active instructors. In five short years, Valley-Hi Lodge was down to one instructor, and in 2020, the last certified instructor was in a severe car accident. With him sidelined indefinitely, the lodge has scrambled to support the Entered Apprentices and Fellow Craft Masons. Encourage all capable Masons to learn what it takes to be a mentor and take the time to learn the esoteric work because anything can happen to the few Brothers working hard to teach the Masonic education in your lodge. If we do a poor job of teaching the Blue Lodge's future leaders, then we can be assured there will be poor leadership.[35]

Being the Lead Learner

"The role of the Worshipful Master is to guide and protect the lodge as well as instruct the members."[36] In context, Brother Poll's statement referenced the qualification of a Worshipful Master. Instructing the members does not mean that the top leader of the Blue Lodge has to know everything, but it does mean he must be a lead learner. The Worshipful Master should attend Masonic workshops, be present for education nights, seek light outside the lodge, and encourage the Brethren to do the same. The internet and smartphone technology opened the door for anyone to gain knowledge from the palm of their hand. There is no need to spend hours away from your home in some dusty old library to gain additional light. There is no reason that a Worshipful Master can't pursue a topic of interest and then pass that knowledge to their lodge. You are modeling for the Brethren how to seek and apply education to their daily lives and adding value to your lodge.

Podcasts

What is a podcast? Think of talk radio or maybe even the old radio shows from the 1950s. They can be about any topic or nothing in particular. Anyone can start a podcast at little to no cost. This is important to keep in mind because quality may vary. A couple of the most popular Masonic podcasts are The Masonic Round Table and the Whence Came You Podcast. The Masonic Round Table is comprised of a few Brothers who pick a topic to cover each week. From time to time, they have a guest who will visit the show. Brother Robert Johnson hosts the Whence Came You Podcast. Each week, Brother Johnson will read a few published Masonic papers. The benefit of listening to a podcast is that you can do so on-demand and search past episodes for a topic that catches your interest.

Worshipful Masters can encourage lodge members to listen to podcasts by including links in the monthly newsletter, emailing links to their favorite episodes, or sharing episodes via text messages. Adventurous lodge leaders may consider starting a lodge podcast. Several apps will allow a podcaster to record right from their phone at no cost. Anchor is a podcasting app that is incredibly easy to use. For those that are technology savvy, download a free audio editor like Audacity to edit your podcast for a cleaner product to publish to your listeners. Once posted, share the link to your podcast with all your members.

Start with something simple like discussing lodge news and then move to interview Past Masters of your lodge. Not only will your members who are no longer able to attend stated meetings or events be able to reengage, but this will also become a record for your Blue

Lodge history. In 2020, I started a Masonic podcast called Perfect Ashlar Podcast with Brother Jon Hudson. We started the podcast to review books on topics surrounding Freemasonry. Listeners can hear the podcast at https://anchor.fm/perfectashlar.

Like an audiobook, listening to a podcast is a great way to learn something new about Masonry while you are stuck in traffic or on your way to work. Most podcasts are available on multiple platforms and apps. Typically, a listener will be able to download a podcast to their smartphone and then play it in their car using Bluetooth technology. All podcasts can be played from a desktop or laptop computer using home internet technology. In 2020, there were just over 30 Masonic podcasts. See the list of known Masonic Podcasts in Figure 23.

Brother-Compiled List of Masonic Podcasts[37]

Name	Website
357 Masonian	http://357productions.libsyn.com/
After Lodge	https://www.afterlodge.com/
Austin Light	https://www.facebook.com/groups/austinfreemasons/
Brother the Masonic Podcast	https://player.fm/series/brother-the-masonic-podcast
Brought to Light	http://podcast.blueloungesc.com/
Contemplative Builder	https://chuckdunning.com/
Follow Me	https://www.youtube.com/followmemasonic
Fort Worth 148	https://directory.libsyn.com/shows/view/id/fortworth148
Freemasonry in the Bakken	https://www.bakkenmasons.com/

Front Porch Masonic	https://frontporchpodcast357.libsyn.com/
Historical Light	https://www.historicallight.com/
In the Chair	https://masonicpodcast.com/
Masonic Central	https://www.blogtalkradio.com/masonic-central
Masonic Improvement	https://www.youtube.com/channel/UCnKjPlQhBbSNSDwK2ljmKRw
Masonic Life 360	https://anchor.fm/masoniclife360
Masonic Lite	https://www.masoniclite.com/
Masonic Radio Theater	http://mrt.uponthesquare.com/
Masonic Wages	https://masonicwages.com/podcast-357/
Meet, Act, and Part	https://podtail.com/en/podcast/meet-act-and-part/
Rocky Mountain Mason	https://rockymountainmason.buzzsprout.com/
Perfect Ashlar Podcast	https://anchor.fm/perfectashlar
Scottish Rite Journal	https://www.spreaker.com/show/scottish-rite-journal-podcast
Solomon's Staircase	https://anchor.fm/sslodge357/
The Craftsmen	http://www.thecraftsmenpodcast.com/
The Laudable Pursuit	https://www.thelaudablepursuit.com/podcast
The Life Masonic	https://www.stitcher.com/podcast/life-masonic/the-life-masonic
The Masonic Readers	https://masonicreaders.com/
The Masonic Resurgence	https://masonicresurgence.buzzsprout.com/
The Masonic Roundtable	http://themasonicroundtable.com/
The Winding Stairs	https://www.stitcher.com/podcast/the-winding-stairs

Three Distinct Knocks	https://threedistinctknocks.org/
Tria Prima	https://triaprima.co/tria-prima-podcast/
Tyler's Place	https://scottishrite.org/media-publications/the-tylers-place-podcast/
We Do	https://wedomason.com/
What is a Mason?	http://whatisamason.org/
Whence Came You	https://wcypodcast.com/
Worthy and Well Qualified	https://worthymasonic.libsyn.com/
X-Oriente	https://www.xoriente.com/

Figure 23: List of Masonic Podcasts as of November 2020

Books

There is nothing like having an excellent Masonic book to read and reference anytime the

need arises. For hundreds of years, Masonic leaders, scholars, and philosophers have published their works for Brethren to learn and grow. A search on Amazon will yield thousands of titles to choose from, but the reader will have to sift through the anti-Masonic work to find the genuinely Masonic books. There are a few publishers where a reader can discover Masonic titles; Cornerstone Publishers, McCoy's Masonic Publishing, and Perfect Ashlar Publishing are a few options.

A Worshipful Master should read to be informed on Freemasonry and model for the Brothers of his lodge by being a continuous learner. Reading will lead to fruitful discussions within the Blue Lodge. Worshipful Masters could conduct a book study in the lodge and facilitate a discussion based on the month's lessons. Lodge mentors can assign books to Entered Apprentices, Fellow Crafts, and newly raised Master Masons. Valley-Hi Lodge gives to the Entered Apprentice *Introduction to Freemasonry Volume 1: Entered Apprentice*, the Fellow Craft *Introduction to Freemasonry Volume 2: Fellowcraft*, and the Master Mason *Introduction to Freemasonry Volume 3: Master Mason*. These books by Carl H. Claudy are excellent introductions to the degrees for the candidate. Each candidate is expected to read the books and give a written or oral report to the lodge upon returning their proficiencies.

Every lodge should have a lodge library of books, or at the very least, a list of recommended books (see a list of recommended books towards the end of this book). Keep in mind that our Brothers will seek more light. According to Brother Friedman, the generations coming up are the most educated generation. By 2013, 47% of millennials have post-secondary education and are continually seeking nontraditional platforms to educate themselves.[38] The lodge leadership can guide and feed these hungry young Brothers that are seeking more light. Some Brothers may not like or have the time to read. If that is the case, recommend a podcast or audiobooks to listen to in the car. The important thing is to give the Brethren options to obtain good Masonic education. Finally, allow them to reflect on what they have learned. Reflection is the key to internalizing new learning and has a higher probability of being applied to their daily lives.

Online Meeting Platforms

The 2020 COVID19 pandemic caused a lot of issues for Masonic lodges not being able to meet. It was too dangerous for people to meet in person, which hindered a lodge's ability to continue with face-to-face education programs. However, like many schools worldwide, Masonic lodges had to think outside the box to continue with their Masonic education.

The dangers of a worldwide pandemic impacted how we could meet as Masons. While before the year 2020, Freemasonry was hesitant to be innovative and move from face-to-face meetings to Internet platforms. However, something beautiful began to happen when Masons were forced to look at alternative means to how they meet. Masonic leaders worldwide began to host nightly discussions, social meet-ups, and education nights through online meeting platforms, like Google Meets and Zoom. In some cases, state Grand Lodges began to host Grand communications through the same online venues and even used apps to conduct Grand Lodge voting.

Masonic lodges meeting on the internet is not entirely a new concept. For years, Castle Island Virtual Lodge in Canada has met in an online tiled lodge format with its members worldwide. Castle Island has a special dispensation to host online tiled lodges; most Grand Lodges will not allow tiled internet events.

During the COVID19 lockdown, Valley-hi Lodge hosted a weekly education night through an online platform meeting. These meet-ups were a non-tiled event that allowed Brothers to meet and participate in other lodge members' presentations on Masonic education topics. Topics ranged from different readings, presentations on how the speaker applied Freemasonry to their life, and discussions on notable Freemasons throughout history. Not only were these events educational in nature, but they also allowed for Brothers to connect during a time when we couldn't leave the house. One Valley-Hi Lodge member, Brother Tim Long, noted that through the weekly internet education events, he learned so much about Freemasonry in such a short amount of time. He felt that he received more Masonic education during the COVID19 quarantine than any other time during his 20-year history as a member. Additionally, he thought that the experience of connecting and being online with other Brothers was invaluable. Many Brothers encouraged the online meetings to continue even after the lockdown had lifted.

An unintended consequence of hosting these online meetings was that Valley-Hi Lodge connected with members from around the world that had not engaged in the lodge for a very long time. There were approximately 115 members at Valley-Hi Lodge in 2020, and only 25% of those members were actively attending the lodge. Many members lived across the world. Each online education night was recorded and then uploaded to YouTube on a private channel. Every Valley-Hi Lodge member received a link to the videos by email. One lodge member lived in a different time zone in Spain and could not attend live online, but he anticipated a new video link each week.

In March 2020, Valley-Hi Lodge planned and scheduled a Masonicon event. A Masonicon is a conference with various speakers. Sticking with the third goal theme of education, this would be an education event and a fundraiser for Valley-Hi Lodge. For this one-day event, six Masonic speakers were scheduled to speak on various topics surrounding Freemasonry. Unfortunately, the COVID19 pandemic caused a quarantine across the United States, which prevented the event from happening. It was rescheduled for October 2020 in hopes that the pandemic would be under control. By August, it was clear that COVID19 was still making it unsafe to travel, so it looked like the lodge would have to cancel the event.

The experience Valley-Hi Lodge had using online meeting platforms to host education meet-ups in the Spring gave the members the confidence to host a virtual Masonicon event instead of the preplanned face-to-face event. During the virtual Masonicon, eight Masonic speakers presented to approximately 30 ticketholders from across the United States and Canada. Each presentation was recorded, securely stored, and shared with all participants and ticketholders. Lodges can use online meeting platforms to connect their members, host fundraising events with speakers, or provide educational opportunities by creating workshops that can raise money for the lodge.

Worshipful Masters and lodge leaders should consider setting up an inexpensive online meeting tool account for their lodge to connect members through online education meet-ups and/or social events. Consider recording videos and uploading them to a private YouTube account that will allow you to share news and events with members who have not engaged in your lodge. Even though members may not often come to the lodge, they still pay dues or are endowed members in your lodge.

Once again, lodge members are customers, and they deserve a quality product. Consider what product your lodge is providing to the members and how you can improve it. Using online tools like Google Meets, Zoom, and YouTube are great examples of how you can enhance your members' lodge experience.

Esoteric Work

Manly P. Hall stated that "True Freemasonry is esoteric."[39] Based on that quote, our esoteric work is vital to our craft. Therefore, each Worshipful Master must ensure that the integrity of the esoteric work rises to the level of expectations of the builders of the past. It is what our founding fathers practiced and kept so close to their hearts over 300 years ago. It is critical that Blue Lodge leadership protects it and ensure its reverence and accuracy. The esoteric work is at the foundation of Freemasonry.

Have you ever been in the lodge with a visitor, and something goes wrong with the esoteric work? When initiating a new Brother or raising a new Master Mason, has the esoteric delivery been sub-par, leading to embarrassment? Many times, this happens because lodges have long periods of dry spells between degrees. They do not come together to practice the degrees, or the degree team is thrown together with little to no preparation. Moments like these, you can see the experienced Brothers in the room begin to sink in their chairs as a VIP visitor or a Brother from another lodge bears witness from the sidelines.

To avoid these embarrassing scenarios and maintain the reputation of the Blue Lodge, Worshipful Masters need to ensure that the esoteric work is taken seriously. They should schedule practice sessions to run through degree work and opening and closing the lodges. Invite Brothers from surrounding lodges known to be proficient in the esoteric work. Ask them to mentor your lodge. Seek support from the district education officer if members are not proficient in their esoteric work. Ensure the degree team practices and studies their part. Pick degree team members who you can count on to know their role. Always have Brothers who can be backups just in case there is an emergency on the day of the degree. Advanced planning and preparation by the lodge will avoid needing to fill a position on the day of the degree. We owe it to the candidate to ensure that he has the best possible experience.

It is essential that the opening and closing of the lodge and degrees are practiced and performed by proficient Brothers. Still, it is equally important that the mentors for the candidates who are going through the degrees know the esoteric work meaning. It is invaluable to our newest Brothers to learn the importance of the esoteric work while they are memorizing their catechism. Not only will they be able to remember the memory work easier, but they will also be able to internalize it and become better Masons. A strong mentorship program focused on applying the esoteric knowledge that our founding fathers were so passionate about will keep the newest and youngest Masons engaged in the craft and your lodge.

Some may feel that the Worshipful Master must be fully proficient in all the esoteric work. However, considering that everybody is different and may not have the capacity to memorize the lodges' opening and closing and conduct all three Masonic degrees, it is crucial that the Worshipful Master has a strong working knowledge of the esoteric work and does not necessarily have it all memorized. They need to be fully proficient in opening and closing the four lodges (EA, FC, MM, and Lodge of Sorrow) before getting to the East. There will be bystanders on the sidelines that will be critical of the Worshipful Master, who cannot proficiently open and close their lodge, impacting his overall leadership credibility.

Having a strong foundation of the esoteric work will allow the Worshipful Master to monitor and instruct other Brothers to facilitate esoteric education. One of the first tasks that a Worshipful Master should do upon his installation is establishing a comprehensive lodge education program that includes a strong foundation in Masonic esoteric work.

Chapter 8

Heavy is the Crown

"Uneasy is the head that wears a crown."

– Henry IV – William Shakespeare.

Many pressures come with being the leader of a Blue Lodge. One has to wonder if the term for an installed Worshipful Master is only one calendar year because of the amount of stress it can take to efficiently run a lodge. Once the Worshipful Master has officially been installed and the lodge contact list is updated, he can be called upon at any time and for any reason concerning the lodge. He will be approached by members, officers, Past Masters, and Grand Lodge representatives. The Worshipful Master will face decisions that the lodge may or may not have dealt with in the past. Brothers who have an opinion on how he should manage each situation will voice their ideas and concerns to him. Keeping in focus the members, the lodge's stability, and careful consideration for the lodge's future when making decisions will ensure that the Worshipful Master reaches the best possible decision.

Lodge Officers

One of the most critical elements of a Worshipful Master's success will be his lodge officers. Officers need to support him and be engaged in implementing the goals and overall operations to move the lodge forward. As mentioned in the previous chapters, all the

Lodge officers must be on the same page with the lodge goals and mission for that year and future years. If any of the officers is not on board with the year's identified goals and does not show up ready to work, is absent from scheduled activities, or is disengaged, it will be a challenging year for the Worshipful Master to succeed. He will be doing two jobs instead of one. Unfortunately, the Worshipful Master does not necessarily get to pick his officers.

While he is progressing through the chairs, the Worshipful Master needs to connect and build relationships with all the progressive line officers. When sitting in the East, he will depend on those officers to assist him in running the lodge. Without good relationships with these officers, it will not be easy to lead them. Before going into the East, if there is an officer who appears to be missing meetings and not participating in lodge activities, it is crucial to discuss with that Brother his commitment to the lodge to ensure that he is still willing to meet his responsibilities in that role. Sometimes, Brothers have changes in job status, family dynamics, and motivation. In this case, the Brother should be encouraged to step out of the line until their situation improves, and he can refocus on the lodge.

The two most essential officers to a Worshipful Master are the secretary and treasurer. In many cases, these two positions have Brothers who have served in that role for several years. Sometimes, Brothers may become complacent or comfortable in that position and may not be putting the amount of effort into it that they did in years past. It may be critical for the Worshipful Master to nominate a different member to fulfill those duties during his year. Both positions in Texas are elected, but anyone can be nominated to be the treasurer or secretary. It is highly recommended that the person be a Past Master. One consideration is for a treasurer and secretary to only serve for two to three years, and a Junior Past Master serves the lodge in one of those roles for up to a three-year term. A Brother who has been in that office for ten years may be adequately fulfilling his responsibilities. The incoming Worshipful Master and Brothers of the lodge will need to assess.

Incoming Worship Masters should talk to and listen to their potential officers before the election night. In the case of Valley-Hi Lodge, one of the lodge's critical officers informed the Senior Warden that he would most likely not fulfill that position or role going into the following Masonic year. The Senior Warden convinced the Brother to accept the nomination for at least one more year, and he would, in turn, take that office once he was a Junior Past Master. Two months after the election, the Brother moved away from the lodge and was unable to fulfill his role. Valley-Hi Lodge had to get a dispensation from the Grand Master of Texas to appoint a different Brother to that position three months after the installation. It is highly recommended that the Worship Master has conversations with each Brother that will be in each officer position in his year and listen to their responses. He should go with his gut before making any nominations during the election. This will save a lot of work and heartache during his year in the East.

It should be noted that electioneering is not allowed by the Grand Lodge of Texas and most likely is not authorized by other Grand Lodges. Therefore, the incoming Worship Master needs to tread lightly and speak hypothetically when discussing current and potential future officer positions—for example, stating, "If I am honored to be nominated and elected to be Worshipful Master." Or saying, "If you are nominated and duly elected by the Brothers, would you serve as my Junior Deacon?"

He should never ask members of the lodge to vote for a particular Brother based on the potential new Worshipful Master's recommendation. In the next section, we will dive a little deeper into the progressive line within a Blue Lodge and why sitting in the progressive line should never guarantee an officer spot for the following year.

Progressive Line

Within the Blue Lodge, certain officer positions are considered part of a progressive line to the East. These officer positions typically are the Junior Steward, Senior Steward, Junior Deacon, Senior Deacon, Junior Warden, Senior Warden, and finally ending with the Worshipful Master. The progressive line refers to the notion that any Brother sitting in one officer position will automatically progress to the next officer post the following Masonic year. Some Masons feel that this line is a tradition that should continue year after year. Yet, officer positions are nominated by a member and then voted on, requiring a majority vote from the Brethren, indicating that the Blue Lodge leadership is a democracy.

A Brother nominated and elected into any of the officer positions, more especially the Worshipful Master position, should be an honor to serve—a distinction which should not just be handed down to the next Brother in line. The nomination and election process are in place to protect the lodge from having an officer with poor intentions or an ineffective Brother fill that position. As a

Brother moves through the chairs, this is equivalent to a job interview. The lodge members should be watching the Brother's actions and his skill set to best evaluate his potential as the future leader of that lodge.

In the business world, leaders are relieved of their responsibilities and duties due to a lack of performance. Sometimes a person is very effective in their position; then, something happens in their personal life or work environment that changes their approach or work productivity. When this happens, serious consideration should be made concerning whether that person is appropriate for the next officer position. The Blue Lodge stakes are too high to have ineffective leadership. They are volunteer organizations that can be very difficult to manage; therefore, members should ensure that they nominate and elect the appropriate person for any leadership position. It'll be much more challenging to remove an unsuccessful officer than not to select a potentially poor one.

It may be a tradition for the officers sitting in a station or place to nominate his successor. A Brother should never feel pressured to nominate another member that he does not think fits the position. Ultimately, after serving in that chair, he knows what the job requires and who can be successful. He is free to put forward anyone who is a member of that lodge to any post. Likewise, any other lodge member can nominate a different Brother of their choosing. Therefore, on election night, if there is a Brother that the incoming Worshipful Master feels is a better fit for the officer lineup for his year, he should feel comfortable enough to nominate any Brother he sees fit. And when there is more than one member of the lodge nominated for a position, the lodge will allow democracy to play out. The Brethren will vote their conscience to decide who to elect.

Past Masters

Past Masters are a critical component of every Blue Lodge. They are the only members of your lodge that most likely have sat in every officer position within the progressive line, and they certainly have experience as a Worshipful Master. Past Masters will provide guidance, expertise, and insight that he has yet to have as a Blue Lodge leader. While sitting in the East, the first-time Worshipful Master should seek advice from all Past Masters. However, always remember that as Worshipful Master, you make the final decision, and the decision should be based on what is best for the Brethren and the lodge.

Before election night, the Senior Warden will be approached by Past Masters, who will voice their concerns about the lodge and try to give pointers on his upcoming year. Of course, all these suggestions are made through hypothetical situations because the full membership body elects the Worshipful Master, not a few Past Masters. Each Past Master have their agendas and has unique experiences in and out of the lodge. Respect the counsel of the lodge Past Masters, but after careful consideration and referring to the lodge bylaws, the Grand Lodge laws, and final consultation with your officers, then should you make a ruling.

Keep the Past Masters involved and engaged in the Blue Lodge. Don't be afraid to ask for advice and consultation. Always explain your Why behind making decisions. Keep your word and show them that you will act upon what you say. Be transparent with the Past Masters. If you make a mistake (You Will), admit it and tell them how you plan to fix it for the future. Show the Past Masters that you are fair and unbiased in your leadership of the Blue Lodge. Do this, and they will have your back and support you. You will earn their respect based on your actions and by returning that same respect to the Past Masters, Brethren, your Blue Lodge, and Freemasonry as a whole.

Full Responsibility

There many responsibilities that a Worshipful Master has as the leader of the Blue Lodge. He must protect the Charter, ensure that the lodge is following and meeting the requirements laid out by the Grand Lodge of their state, and he has full responsibility for the lodge. Meaning that any action that the lodge takes, or his officers take, the full responsibility for those actions rests on the Worshipful Master. When agreeing to serve in the East, the Brother must be fully prepared for the difficulties that may come his way during his year.

During the 2019–2020 Masonic Year I faced various challenges as Worshipful Master. I had a critical officer to the lodge that did not show up for the first two months after the installation. Then that officer resigned his position. Keep in mind that in Texas, officers technically cannot quit. The Grand Master of Texas needed to issue a special dispensation to allow the lodge to appoint a new Brother to that position.

During the audit, the audit committee raised some concerns regarding missing or vague documentation. There was a lodge break-in soon after questions were raised, and several warrants and receipts went missing. I received pressure from Past Masters, who wanted action taken regarding the audit and break-in. They guided me through contacting the Grand Lodge of Texas to investigate what had happened. The audit committee could not finish the audit on time without the proper paperwork, so I requested from the Grand Lodge an extension to complete the audit. Eventually, the guidance came down that the lodge had to approximate the amount of spending, even though the organization could not correctly report how the funds were spent without the warrants and receipts. The Grand Lodge was unable to return an answer regarding the investigation until nearly a month later. This incident led to changes to our lodge's overall checks and balances and resulted in an update to the Valley-Hi Lodge procedures.

The newly appointed officer for that critical position did an excellent job. He was able to reorganize that position's duties and streamline how that position supported the lodge. Unfortunately, after being in that position for only a few months, the Brother was in a major car accident on the way to the lodge to mentor an Entered Apprentice. He survived the accident but required surgery to fuse some vertebrae in his spine. After the surgery, he discovered some heart complications due to the accident and was out for the remainder of the year. I had to find a pro tem officer for that position. While I could find someone to fill in during each stated meeting, I could not find a permanent replacement and had to do some of the duties that the position required. The car accident was a horrific event for the Brother and his family. Still, it serves as an example of how the Worshipful Master has to step up and ensure that every officer position's duties continue. Lodge operations do not stop when a Brother is unable to fulfill those requirements. It falls on the Worshipful Master to ensure it gets done, even if that means he has to do it himself.

A building committee was assigned to supervise the Valley-Hi Lodge renovations done by the community college. The Brothers in charge of that project were doing a fantastic job. Things were going well until COVID19 hit the country hard. When that happened, all schools closed down, including the community college. The lodge's work would not be completed until the lockdown is lifted, leaving Valley-Hi Lodge with several refurbishment projects not complete. Myself and several other Brothers worked from home during this time allowing for flexibility to meet at the lodge and continue the community college's work. The Brothers came together and worked outside the lodge, painting it, cleaning up, and taking off the graffiti. On the inside, they repainted the lodge waiting area and put the toilets, vanities, and mirrors into the bathrooms. They also cleaned up and repainted the anteroom. The work these Brothers completed was critical because the lodge reopened before the school. Valley-Hi Lodge was able to have stated meetings and conduct degree work. Without organizing these activities, the lodge would most likely not have been operational before the Brothers returned.

When COVID19 hit, and the country was in lockdown, Entered Apprentice Masons and their mentors could not meet to practice their memory work. Additionally, the Brother who was in the car accident was our only lodge mentor. I took on two Entered Apprentice Masons. Another Brother took on one, and together, they ensured that the three Brothers were ready to return their memory work as soon as the lodge opened back up. They worked with the younger Entered Apprentice Masons over the phone nearly every day during the lockdown. Without taking the initiative to ensure that these Brothers were ready, it would have significantly delayed their progress. Possibly, the Brothers would have disengaged and given up on their work altogether. Now, all three are Master Masons.

During the lockdown, I also started a weekly education night using an online meeting platform to connect Brothers and to continue Masonic education. I organized the meeting each week, asked Brothers to present, created presentations, uploaded the videos to YouTube, and emailed the lodge members links to the presentations. This took a lot of work and time for the me to complete. Eventually, other Brothers took on the responsibility of hosting the education night; unfortunately, it did not have the same participation. Sometimes the business of the daily grind gets in the way of our Masonic participation. Something I am also guilty of neglecting.

Modeling Leadership

Since the Blue Lodge is a volunteer organization, it will be difficult for the Worshipful Master to get anything done if he does not empower and motivate his lodge members to take the initiative in various activities. While some Brothers are quick to help, many will not take the initiative without the Worshipful Master first giving them a nudge to get something done. If the Worshipful Master is not consistent at activities or does not ensure that time is scheduled to do lawn maintenance on the lodge, have cleanup parties, or schedule education nights, these operational items will not get done. It is imperative that the Worshipful Master models leadership for his subordinate officers and the lodge Brethren.

Modeling High Expectations

A few years ago, a mentor from my usual vocation advised, "Dress for the job that you want." He was a principal and dressed like a high-level school district executive by wearing a tailored three-piece suit. Today, he is an assistant superintendent. My mentor was trying to instill in me that dressing up communicated a level of respect. Blue Lodge officers who frequently dress up and wear a jacket and tie for special events will have an easier time being seen by the Brethren as people who should be respected. It not only communicates authority but also informs the Brothers that running a lodge is serious business. An added benefit is that other members will begin to mirror their leadership and dress up too.

Modeling high expectations at times will require dealing with uncomfortable situations. One of the most challenging tasks for a candidate is returning the catechism in the middle of a stated meeting with a room full of Master Masons who know the memory work. There were two occasions during the 2019–2020 Masonic Year when I stopped a candidate's question and answer demonstration because the Brothers were making several mistakes. Each one of the candidates was adequately prepared, but sometimes, the nerves kick in. It would have been easy for me to allow them to finish and let the lodge vote on the return. However, respectfully intervening and assuring the Brothers that they could continue to prepare to give their return at a future date provided them both with relief.

On one occasion, a visitor at our stated meeting witnessed how the uncomfortable catechism was handled. The visitor commented on how he was impressed with the stoppage and was glad to see that Valley-Hi Lodge respected the esoteric rite of passage that each candidate must become proficient. Both the candidates mentioned above also were appreciative for ending their return early. The act prevented them from continued embarrassment, and it allowed them the opportunity to showcase later that they were truly prepared. Both candidates returned the following month and successfully gave their returns, which were near word-perfect.

Whether it is stopping a Brother who struggles during their catechism return or dropping the gavel during a heated debate, it can be uncomfortable to do what needs to be done as a Worshipful Master. It is in these awkward moments that we grow as leaders. These moments are opportunities to model for our Blue Lodge's future leaders and possibly change the course of our fraternity. High expectations for ourselves and our lodge are the catalyst to improvement. Years of lowering expectations and allowing for subpar work will harm morale, a lodge's reputation, and its overall productivity. Changing the direction starts with the Worshipful Master, who sets the expectations and leads by example.

A Call to Action

"Courage is the first of human qualities, because it is the quality which guarantees all the others."

– Brother Winston Churchill.

When called upon by your Brothers, it takes courage to lead. Do not let fear hinder your leadership. Allow for your experiences and the good counsel of your Brethren to shine like a beacon of light in the darkness of uncertainty. When faced with challenges, listen to those who have come before you, seek additional light, and reflect on what you have learned. Listen to your heart and allow your mind to steer you in the right direction. The best possible decisions for your lodge will bring you peace. Be wary of the angst that will be a warning in the pit of your stomach. When present, seek further counsel or reflection before finalizing a decision.

While it may be challenging to take the steps necessary to apply the innovative strategies outlined in this book, you have a moral obligation to do what is essential to keep your Blue Lodge open. Your Blue Lodge should be a beacon in your community, guiding men to become better husbands, fathers, sons, employees, and citizens. Our fraternity has given so much to you over the years. Now, it is your turn to use the gifts the Grand Architect of the Universe has endowed in you to make a real difference in the world. Take what you have learned, use the platform that your Brethren have entrusted to you to lead your Blue Lodge into the remainder of the 21st century by

Leading From the East

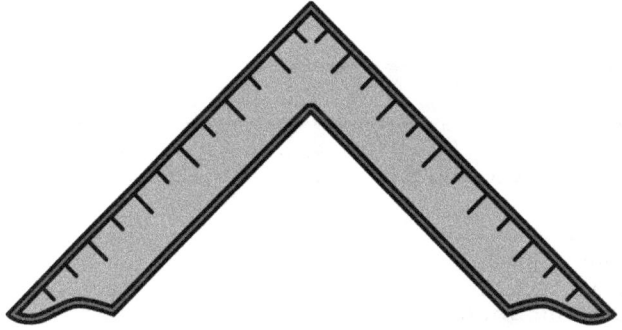

Recommended Reading List

Title/Description	Author/Notes
Overall Leadership	
Start With Why	Simon Sinek
Leaders Eat Last	Simon Sinek
Multipliers: How the Best Leaders Make Everyone Smarter	Liz Wiseman
Developing the Leader Within You	John C. Maxwell
Good to Great	Jim Collins
Lincoln on Leadership: Executive Strategies for Tough Times	Donald T. Phillips
Degrees	
Introduction to Freemasonry Volumes 1, 2 & 3	Carl H. Claudy
New Master	
Lodge Leadership Program	Your Grand Lodge
Monitor of the Lodge	Your Grand Lodge
Grand Lodge Law Book	Your Grand Lodge
Introduction to Freemasonry Volume 3	Carl H. Claudy
Member	
Ancient Manuscripts of the Freemasons	Michael R. Poll

A Pilgrim's Path; One Man's Road to the Masonic Temple	John J. Robinson
A Pilgrim's Path; Freemasonry and the Religious Right	John J. Robinson
Anderson's Constitution of 1723 &1738	James Anderson & W.J. Hughan
I Just Didn't Know That	Rev. Neville Barker Cryer
Famous American Freemasons (Volumes 1 & 2)	Todd E. Creason
House Undivided	Allen E. Roberts
The Better Angels of our Nature	Michael A. Halleran
Revolutionary Brotherhood	Steven C. Bullock
Freemasonry In American History	Allen E. Roberts
The Liverpool Masonic Rebellion and the Wigan Grand Lodge	David Harrison
Principles of Masonic Law – Treatise on Constitutional Laws	Albert G. Mackey
Is It True What They Say About Freemasonry?	Art DeHoyos & S. Brent Morris
Lexicon of Freemasonry	Albert G. Mackey
The Red Triangle; A History of Anti-Masonry	Robert L.D. Cooper
Morgan; The Scandal that Shook Freemasonry	Stephan Dafoe
Blue Lodge Officer	
Grand Lodge Law Book	Your Grand Lodge

The Master's Book	Carl H. Claudy
Principles of Masonic Law – Treatise on Constitutional Laws	Albert G. Mackey
Monitor of the Lodge	Your Grand Lodge
Past Master	
Mackey' Encyclopedia of Freemasonry	Albert G. Mackey
The Symbolism of Freemasonry	Albert G. Mackey
Coils Masonic Encyclopedia	Henry Wilson Coil & W. Brown
Millennial Freemasonry: The Next Revolution in Freemasonry	Samuel Friedman

About the Author

Brother Chris Galloway is the Past Master of Valley-Hi Lodge #1407. As Worshipful Master, he applied his business and organizational leadership knowledge to a very successful year for his lodge. He is a full member of the Texas Lodge of Research, the San Antonio Scottish Rite, and the Helotes Chapter and Council. In 2024, Brother Galloway was appointed as the Chairman for the Grand Lodge of Texas Committee on Masonic Education.

Brother Galloway was raised in January 2015 at Valley-Hi Lodge #1407 in San Antonio, TX. When raised, he worked as a teacher/coach for a San Antonio, TX high school. Since becoming a Master Mason, Brother Galloway has successfully moved from teacher to superintendent of a Texas school district. He completed his Ph.D. in School Improvement from Texas State University and now teaches doctoral classes in the same program. He credits his success to his application of the tenants of Freemasonry to his life. Brother Galloway is married to his wife, Kimberly, and has three beautiful children: Gabriella, Thomas, and Aubrielle.

Brother Galloway is passionate about growing leaders in Freemasonry and the educational field. He started a publishing company, Perfect Ashlar Publishing, to help other authors spread their message to the world. Brother Galloway loves to hear from his readers. He can be reached at www.perfectashlarpublishing.com.

A NOTE TO THE READER

Thank you for purchasing and reading my book! I hope that this book has inspired you and has become a valuable addition to your Masonic library. If you have enjoyed this book, please consider leaving an honest review on your favorite online bookstore website.

As a special thank you for reading this book, please head to www.perfectashlarpublishing.com to access free content and to stay up to date with our latest news.

Check out these Masonic books from Perfect Ashlar Publishing

Leading from the East: Innovative Strategies for Masonic Lodges

By Christophor Galloway, PM

For over 200 years, Masonic scholars have written about the need for innovation in Freemasonry to "save our fraternity." Within the pages of Leading From the East, resources and strategies will help Blue Lodge leaders identify their vision, attract new members from several different generations, and engage the new members who join. Additionally, the very same strategies will bring back those Brothers who have disengaged from our Craft. A Worshipful Master implemented the strategies presented in this book at a Blue Lodge that was in jeopardy of closing its doors forever and now that same lodge has a bright future. Finally, this book is also a call to action that Masonic leaders must take a new approach to keep Freemasonry around for another 300 years.

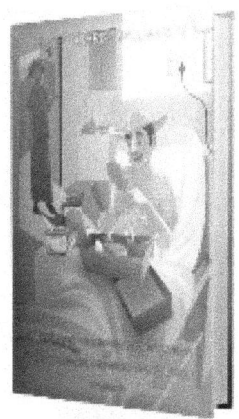

The Profound Pontifications of Big John Deacon, Freemason Extraordinaire

Volume I – IV

By James "Chris" Williams IV, PM

Brother Big John Deacon is a larger-than-life Texas Freemason and Past Master. He towers at 6 feet 7 inches tall and weighs in at 275 pounds. People seem to always notice him in his black alligator boots and 7X Stetson Silverbelly cowboy hat.

He commands attention when he walks into a room with his plain-spoken and exuberant personality. Brother Chris Williams met him several years ago when Brother Deacon's large black F-350 pick-up truck needed repairs. Brother Williams has authentically captured Big John's gruff but gentle cowboy charm and values, which his Masonic membership reinforces. The story of their friendship and adventures is appealing and memorable. Readers may also be familiar with the "Old Tyler's Talks" by Carl H. Claudy, which first appeared in 1921. In many ways, the John Deacon series is a contemporary version of them. Within the pages of each book, there is a pearl of folksy wisdom that is timeless. Brother Deacon is a mix of walking (and mechanical) disasters and knowledge born of passion and profound reflections on Freemasonry and today's Lodge challenges. The John Deacon book series will have readers laughing, crying, and, more importantly, reflecting on Freemasonry.

There is No Texas Without Freemasonry: A Collection of Short Writings on Masonry

By James "Chris" Williams IV, PM

Within the covers of this book is a collection of Masonic papers written over the last twenty-five years by Brother Williams. Most of them have been presented at various Masonic and non- Masonic gatherings. There is No Texas Without Freemasonry is the first and most famous paper presented to date by Brother Williams. This book is an excellent addition to any Masonic library. Each chapter is short enough to be read as an education piece in the Lodge or as the focus of family education night. Enjoy each page as you laugh, cry, and, more importantly, reflect on Freemasonry.

Light Reflections: Philosophical Thoughts and Observations of a Texas Freemason

By Bradley E. Kohanke, PM

Freemasonry in the United States was arguably at its peak during the decade following the first World War. The Masonic writings of the day were eloquent, easy to read, concise, and filled with thought-provoking opinions and observations. This was the model after which Bradley E. Kohanke patterned his writings. For nearly 10 years, Brother Kohanke, a Past Master, former District Deputy Grand Master, and former Grand Orator for the Grand Lodge of Texas wrote a monthly article for his Lodge's newsletter.

Also included are his Orations from the Texas Grand Lodge Historical Observances in 2019 and his Grand Oration from the Grand Annual Communication in January of 2020. As Brother Kohanke puts it:

Masonry holds no secrets or sacred knowledge that are suddenly revealed to the initiate. Rather, it provides a framework on which to build…a guide for living. It offers a way to attain that knowledge over time through learning, patience, and truth. And it does so without harming others in their search. This practice of perfecting one's self is ancient beyond record and is the true measure of success. The attainment of balance in one's life…achieving happiness with yourself, without interfering with the happiness of others, and proactively helping others in their search for balance in their lives…that is success.

It is a noble quest, the objective of which can only truly be obtained by those who are worthy and true…to themselves and each other. Good luck on your quest, and enjoy it.

"Masonic duty is to learn and to teach others."

Brotherhood of God:
A Book of Masonic Prayers
By Garron C. Daniels

Brotherhood of God is a collection of prayers to be used by Freemasons, used both within the Lodge and in daily life. It is an aid for the spiritual needs of the Fraternity to remind all of the importance of God in all that we do.

Garron C. Daniels is a Freemason from the State of Missouri. He's a member of Brotherhood Lodge #269 in St Joseph, Mo, a member of the Scottish Rite and York Rite, and several other fundraising bodies of Freemasonry.

He gains his influence in writing from his studies about the Fraternity as well as his studies in becoming an Episcopal Priest at the University of the South: School of Theology. He continues to dedicate his time to exploring the religious aspects of Masonry and where Christianity plays a role in it.

Devotion To St. Constantine the Great:

Emperor, Convert, and Devout Follower of Christ

By Garron C. Daniels

Emperor Constantine the Great is a figure that some throughout history have deemed controversial. Yet, his significance and conversion to Christianity have impacted the faith in ways we will never fully understand. While he was a flawed sinner like any other, he still was the primary force that helped bring Christianity from an oppressed faith to being the religion of the Empire. Constantine was truly a Saintly figure who lived to serve not just as an Emperor but as a mere servant to the Almighty. Because of this, we must seriously and sincerely believe that Emperor Constantine the Great should be considered St Constantine, an emperor, convert, and a devout follower of Christ.

A Masons Journey – Noah's Quest:
Volume I: Trial at the Gate
By William H. Boyd

A Mason's Journey – Noah's Quest" Volume I, Trial at the Gate," is a fictional look at a masonic journey, and it is unusual because it starts at an unexpected point in a mason's journey. It is an introduction to Brother Noah Lewis as he reconciles the books of his life and discovers the unseen forces at work, guiding him along his journey. Above all, it contextualizes and illustrates some of the ideas and concepts the author has believed and have described in a variety of other non-fiction vehicles and may, perhaps, be the first in a series intended to animate the tenets of freemasonry through the fictional quest of Brother Noah Lewis. We all have beliefs about our call to accountability and how we may ultimately learn the value of our labors.

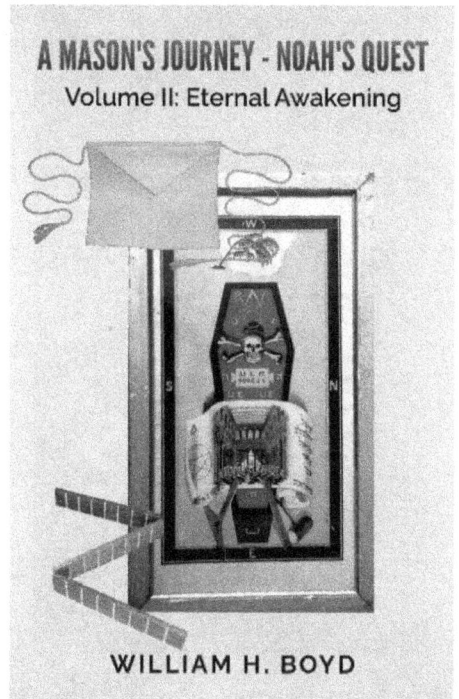

A Masons Journey – Noah's Quest:
Volume II: Eternal Awakening
By William H. Boyd

In book two of the series Noah has come upon The Gate, he had been presented with poignant scenes that were steeped in meaning and were obviously intended to impact him in certain ways. But there was so much he still did not know about this reality and what, if any, control he held. He did not know if or how he should interact with these scenes as they unfolded around him. And he did not know if the scenes were real. Or maybe they were allegories for events from his life gone by? Perhaps they are intended to represent new lessons, meant to teach him further lessons?

A Masons Journey – Noah's Quest:

Volume III: Faithful Craftsman

By William H. Boyd

Brother Noah Lewis continues the quest begun when he unexpectedly finds himself at The Gate in Volume I: "Trial at the Gate." Since his arrival, he has been tested on his ego and self-awareness in preparation for an entirely new journey on an entirely new path.

In Noah's Quest – Volume III: "Faithful Craftsman," Noah begins to see how all of the pieces of his life and his masonic journey fit together in the larger scheme of life on Earth and in eternity. Noah learns a valuable lesson on the passage of time and the immortality of the soul.

In and About the Lodge

By William H. Boyd

In his second excursion into non-fiction, Brother William H. Boyd explores the lodge's role in the masonic experience. He examines how it supports the Masonic goal of "making good men better." He has assembled a collection of articles and blog posts that address how the lodge experience facilitates a man's quest for improvement. The centerpiece of this collection is a particular article titled "A System Called Masonry," it serves as the foundation upon which the other articles are written and represents the bricks of this allegorical edifice.

Lessons From the Craft: Seeing God in Masonic Rituals

By Dr. Douglas Reece

Freemasonry has some of the best practical life lessons contained in our ritual ceremonies. The Great Architect of the Universe inspired me to start my ministry and write down within the pages of this book the lessons I have learned for the benefit of the brethren now and in the future. So, with the guidance of the Holy Spirit, I share with you what I have discovered throughout my search for Christ in the Masonic Ritual. May you find within this book lessons, revelations, meanings, and explanations inspiring enough to start your masonic quest for knowledge and meaning.

Freemasonry and the Divine Comedy

Masonic Commedia

By W.B. Andy Albright

A well-informed Mason is one who tried to improve himself in Masonry as he knows it, applying our generous principles to our lives. If we learn from the great intellectual ancestors, we improve ourselves tremendously as men and masons. Andy Albright has added to the possibility of improvement through his book "Masonic Comedia: Freemasonry and the Divine Comedy." In this well-considered book, Albright weaves a set of narratives linking Dante's "Divine Comedy" to masonic teachings in a practical way.

If you have not read Dante, you will want to after reading Albright's book but will enter into that achievement well-informed and considering more than the simple story that some get from that monumental work. The faithful reader will also reflect more on the lessons he has learned and how they influence everyday life and thoughts of eternal salvation, regardless of that brother's faith tradition. – R.W.Bro. Robert J.F. Elsner, 33°, KYGCH

Share Freemasonry with Future Generations with These Childrens Books

By

Christophor J. Galloway

Notes

[1] Social Issues Research Centre. 2012. "The Future of Freemasonry." http://www.sirc.org/publik/Future_of_Freemasonry.shtml.

[2] Ibid., 36.

[3] Sorkin, Aaron. 2000. *The West Wing: Take This Sabbath Day. Season 1: Episode 14.* Directed by Thomas Schlamme. Performed by Martin Sheen and Karl Malden.

[4] Poll, Michael R. 2018. *A Masonic Evolution: The New World of Freemasonry.* New Orleans, LA: Cornerstone Book Publishers.

[5] Freeman, Doyle. n.d. *Masonic Leadership.* https://www.masonicworld.com/education/articles/masonic_leadership.htm.

[6] Ibid.

[7] Ibid.

[8] Allen GP, Moore WM, Moser LR, Neill KK, Sambamoorthi U, Bell HS. The Role of Servant Leadership and Transformational Leadership in Academic Pharmacy. *Am J Pharm Educ.* 2016;80(7):113. doi:10.5688/ajpe807113

[9] Choi SL, Goh CF, Adam MB, Tan OK. Transformational leadership, empowerment, and job satisfaction: the mediating role of employee empowerment. *Hum Resour Health.* 2016;14(1):73. Published 2016 Dec 1. doi:10.1186/s12960-016-0171-2

[10] Johnson, Robert H, and Jon T Ruark. 2018. *It's Business Time: Adapting a Corporate Path for Freemasonry.* Lexington, KY. This book adapts well known corporate books, like *Who Moved My Cheese?*, *The Challenger Sale*, *The Start-Up*, *The Sales Funnel*, *How to Win Friends and Influence People*, *Too Big To Fail*, and *Think and Grow Rich.*

[11] Sinek, Simon. 2010. "How Great Leaders Inspire Action." May 4. https://www.youtube.com/watch?v=qp0HIF3Sfl4

[12] Sinek, Simon. 2009. *Start With Why: How Great Leaders Inspire Everyone To Take Action.* New York:

[13] Hodapp, Christopher. "Dreaded Doomsayers of Dues." *Freemasons For Dummies*, 1 Sept. 2007, freemasonsfordummies.blogspot.com/2007/08/dreaded-doomsayers-of-dues.html.

[14] Brindle, Nathan C. 2009, "Dues that don't…anymore: Deconstructing Masonic lodge dues myths and fables." http://overseaslodge.com/images/PDFs/6_Dues_That_Dont_Anymore.pdf.

15 Hodapp. 2007. "Dreaded Doomsayers of Dues."

16 Kennedy, Lance. 2018. "Freemasonry Network." *The Decline of Freemasonry: A Data Analysis*. November 29. https://freemasonry.network/more_news/freemasonry-is-dying-the- decline-of-freemasonry-a-data-analysis/.

17 "Masonic Membership Statistics 2016-2017." *Masonic Membership Stats*, www.msana.com/msastats.asp.

18 McCall, Steve. 2018. "41 Million Men." In *41 Million Men: The Importance of the Millenial Generation to Freemasonry*, 19-36. Richmond, VA: Macoy Publishing & Masonic Supply Co., Inc.

19 The Masonic Roundtable Podcast. 2019. *Episode 277 Social Media Marketing*. November 7. Accessed November 1, 2020. https://www.youtube.com/watch?v=CwCsep1t6SA.

20 Grand Lodge of Texas A.F. & A. M. 1982. *Monitor of the Lodge: Monitorial Instructions in the Three Degrees of Symbolic Masonry*. Waco, Texas: Waco Printing Company., 132-133.

21 The Masonic Round Table. 2015. *Episode 84: The Lodge Historian*. September 22. Accessed November 7, 2020. https://www.youtube.com/watch?v=6s5gBkyOwtU. & The Masonic Round Table. 2020. *Episode 319: Keeping Lodge Records Safe*. November 5. Accessed November 7, 2020. https://www.youtube.com/watch?v=qGI8oI0ubmQ.

22 Boyd, William H. 2020. "Lodge History Committee: A paper on suggested responsibilities and duties of a Lodge History Committee." Masonic White Paper., 2-3.

23 Ibid, 3.

24 Mackey, Albert G. 1856. In *The Principles of Masonic Law: A Treatise on The Constitutional Laws, Usages, and Landmarks of Freemasonry*, Chapter 1. New York, NY: JNO. W Leonard & Co., Masonic Publishers.

25 Villa, David. 2018. *How To Overcome Analysis Paralysis*. Forbes. November 19. https://www.forbes.com/sites/forbesagencycouncil/2018/11/19/how-to-overcome-analysis-paralysis/?sh=5b602fa77382.

26 Ibid.

27 Ibid.

28 Angie's List. n.d. *In The Press*. Accessed November 14, 2020. https://www.angieslist.com/in- the-press.htm.

29 Bagley, Mary. 2017. *George Washington Carver: Biography, Inventions & Quotes*. December 7. https://www.livescience.com/41780-george-washington-

carver.html#:~:text=In%20April%201896%2C%20Carver%20received,fame%2C%E2%80%9D%20read%20this%20letter.

[30] Ibid.

[31] Nelson, Matt. 2018. "Education and Seeking Further Light." In *41 Million Men: The importance Generation to Freemasonry*, 57-64. Richmond, VA: Macoy Publishing & Masonic Supply VA: Macoy Publishing & Masonic Supply Company Inc.

[32] Ibid.

[33] Social Issues Research Centre. 2012. "The Future of Freemasonry.", 21.

[34] Ibid., 22.

[35] Poll, Michael R. 2018. *A Masonic Evolution., 124.*

[36] Poll, Michael R. 2019. *A Lodge at Labor: Freemasons and Masonry Today*. New Orleans, LA: Cornerstone Book Publishers., 79.

[37] 2020. *Masonic Podcasts*. August 24. Accessed November 24, 2020. https://github.com/boyer-code/masonic-podcasts.

[38] Friedman, Samuel. 2015. *Millennial Apprentices: The Next Revolution In Freemasonry*. Fairport, NY: Sam Friedman. 70.

[39] Hall, Manly P. n.d. *Freemasonry: The Eternal Quest*. Accessed November 30, 2020. https://www.hermetics.net/media-library/masonic/manly-p-hall-freemasonry-the-eternal-quest/.

www.ingramcontent.com/pod-product-compliance
Lightning Source LLC
Chambersburg PA
CBHW031552040426
42452CB00006B/279